Additional Praise

"I found Hayley's insights truly eye-opening. Her ideas are highly impactful and made me genuinely think differently!"

—Dhiraj Mukherjee
Shazam Co-Founder, Tech Investor,
Leadership & AI Keynote Speaker

"Imagine a world where your voice is heard. Imagine a world where every voice is heard. This is the world that Hayley is seeking to create through her new book. Her own story from her first public speech to captivating international audiences, is why she is the perfect person to share how your message can captivate your audience."

—Russell Findlay
CEO of Speakers Trust, the UK's leading public speaking charity

"Speak Up is more than a message — it's a movement. Hayley's transparency, spiritual depth, and practical wisdom make this a must-read for anyone ready to stop grinding alone and start winning together."

—Carlas "CJ" Quinney
President, Eric Thomas & Associates (ETA)
Multi-Million Personal Brand Builder
Host of The Secrets to Success Podcast

"When Hayley said she wanted to change the world with her voice, she wasn't kidding. In Speak Up, *she outlines exactly how she's been able to do it and how she's made an impact while building a sustainable income from her gift.*

What I've always admired about Hayley is her audacity: her ability to speak the future into the present, her relentless drive, and her tenacity. These qualities have truly impacted the world.

I first met Hayley 18 years ago when she was still in a state of dreams and goals, and to now see her manifest those dreams into reality is nothing short of inspiring. This book is a reflection of her journey, her heart, and her mission and it will help anyone ready to find their voice and change the world."

—Jackson Ogunyemi aka Action Jackson
#1 Youth and School Speaker in Europe

"I had the pleasure of hosting Hayley for a couple of workshops with the Empowering Tribe, and she was absolutely incredible. The way she shares her story, commands the space, and keeps everyone fully engaged from start to finish is truly a masterpiece. I have no doubt that her book will have a huge impact on everyone, to share their story and to speak up!"

—Christine Assouad
CEO of Dublin Donuts Lebanon
Shark/Investor for Shark Tank Lebanon

"Hayley isn't just my friend—she's someone who genuinely lives what she teaches. I've watched her turn her pain into purpose and build bridges across continents, not by chasing platforms but by serving people with her whole heart. 'Speak Up' is exactly what this generation needs—honest, practical, and deeply empowering. She has inspired me and shaped much of my work in so many ways. If you've been waiting for permission to use your voice, stop waiting. Let Hayley show you how to speak up with courage, purpose, and impact. This book is going to be the gift that keeps on giving!"

—Dr. Vee Kativhu
Youngest recipient of an Honorary Doctorate from the University of Bradford, Education Activist, Founder of Empowered By Vee, and Young Leader of the Sustainable Development Goals at the United Nations

"Speak Up is not just a book, it's a reminder that our voices are not accidents but assignments. Hayley's words will inspire you to stop holding back and start speaking up with faith, courage, and conviction."

—Laura Casselman
Wall Street Journal Best-Selling Author, International Speaker, Co-Owner & CEO of JVZoo, a global online marketplace with over $4 billion in sales

SPEAK
UP

FOREWORD BY DR. ERIC THOMAS #1 Motivational Speaker

How to Use Your Voice
to Inspire, Influence, and Earn

SPEAK UP

Hayley Mulenda Record

CAPSTONE
A Wiley Brand

Registered Offices
John Wiley & Sons, Inc., 111 River Street, Hoboken, NJ 07030, USA
John Wiley & Sons Ltd, New Era House, 8 Oldlands Way, Bognor Regis, West Sussex, PO22 9NQ, UK

For details of our global editorial offices, customer services, and more information about Wiley products visit us at www.wiley.com.

The manufacturer's authorized representative according to the EU General Product Safety Regulation is Wiley-VCH GmbH, Boschstr. 12, 69469 Weinheim, Germany, e-mail: Product_Safety@wiley.com.

Wiley also publishes its books in a variety of electronic formats and by print-on-demand. Some content that appears in standard print versions of this book may not be available in other formats.

Library of Congress Cataloging-in-Publication Data is Available:

ISBN 9781907326011 (Paperback)
ISBN 9781907326035 (ePDF)
ISBN 9781907326028 (ePub)

Cover Design: Wiley
Cover Image: © Hey_Alice/Shutterstock
Printed and bound by CPI Group (UK) Ltd, Croydon, CR0 4YY

C9781907326011_031225

To the ones who were told to stay silent.

To the ones who were made to feel small.

To the ones who doubted their voice, their value, or their vision.

This is for you.

You were never too much—you were just around people who couldn't handle your volume.

Speak up. The world needs your sound.

Contents

Foreword

by Dr Eric Thomas

(*New York Times* Bestselling Author of *You Owe You*)

What Up, What Up, What Up!! Listen to me closely. I've been doing this professionally for over 30 years. That's three decades of stages, stadiums, classrooms, and boardrooms. Thirty years of waking up every day and acting like I want to succeed as badly as I want to breathe! But my story didn't start that way. I was a homeless high school dropout who ate out of trash cans on the streets of Detroit, Michigan.

Here's what I've learned from my own journey: People see the mic, but they don't see the seasons of silence—where the real work is done. In my darkest moments, the truth I held on to was found in Scripture. 1 Peter 2:9 says, 'I am a chosen generation, a royal priesthood, a holy nation, God's special possession'. My life taught me that God chose me for this work, and I can't afford to be disobedient. This isn't just a career, it's a calling.

That's why I'm proud to write the foreword for *Speak Up* by Hayley Mulenda Record. Because when I talk about my own calling, I see the same thing in her. Hayley took the blueprint I laid down and didn't just copy it— she made it her own. She applied it, she lived it, and now she's walking in her purpose.

Hayley isn't just a speaker; she's a voice for her generation. She's bold. She's authentic. She's ready. And this book? It's proof. *Speak Up* isn't just a guide to becoming a better communicator—it's a call to become a better person. In a world full of noise, she reminds us that clarity doesn't come from shouting to be heard but from shouting to make a change. This book will help you silence your fears, find your voice, and speak from a place of purpose, not performance, from wholeness, not hustle.

So, if you're ready to stop hiding, to stop playing small, to stop letting fear mute your future ... then this is your moment! Let this book light a fire in you. Let Hayley's words unlock your own. And when you close the final page, I dare you: to speak up.

Now you know, LET'S GO.

Acknowledgements

First and foremost, all glory goes to God. Thank You for giving me the grace to write this book. Thank You for the conviction, the burden, and the call to see people walk in freedom. I didn't write this because it was trendy—I wrote it because You wouldn't let me rest until I did. You whispered when I was weary, corrected me when I drifted, and carried me when I didn't have the words. This book belongs to You. Thank you, Jesus.

To my incredible husband, Sterling Record. You are the answer to prayers I didn't even know how to pray. Thank you for being my safe space, my biggest cheerleader, and my most faithful proofreader. Thank you for staying up with me until 3 a.m. as I typed through tears or overthought every sentence. Your support hasn't just been helpful—it's been healing. I couldn't have done this without you.

To my mum—my anchor and my example. Your prayers, your strength, and your unwavering belief in me have built a foundation I stand on daily. Thank you for being the woman who taught me how to fight battles in the spirit and walk in grace with power. I am who I am because of the seeds you've sown.

To my best friend, Fiona. Thank you for always believing in me—even when my ideas sounded wild. You never laughed at my vision—you leaned in and helped carry it. You've been that one consistent voice reminding me I can, even when I was convinced I couldn't. Your loyalty, your encouragement, and your friendship have meant more than I could ever explain.

And finally—to you, the reader. Thank you for picking up this book. Thank you for taking a chance on your growth, your healing, your voice. I don't take it lightly that you're here. Whether someone handed you this or you picked it up yourself, I believe it found you on purpose. My prayer is that these words won't just inspire you but awaken something within you that's been waiting to rise.

This book wasn't just written for you.

It was written *with* you in mind.

Now that you're about to enter into this book—don't just read it.

Let it read you.

Let the words confront you, comfort you, challenge you, and change you.

This isn't just a book of information—it's an invitation.

To go deeper. To heal. To grow. To speak up.

Don't just highlight sentences—let them highlight parts of you that are ready for breakthrough.

Allow yourself to be transformed.

Because the moment you give yourself permission to fully show up, everything begins to shift.

Your story is still being written.

And I believe the next chapter will be your best one yet.

A Letter to My 15-Year-Old Self

Dear Hayls,

Thank you.

Thank you for the drive.

Thank you for the tenacity.

Thank you for the vision.

Thank you for the hunger.

You didn't even realise it at the time, but every time you chose purpose over popularity, healing over hiding, and obedience over fear—you were breaking generational patterns and building a new path. I owe so much of the life I live now to the boldness of that 15-year-old girl who decided she wasn't going to settle. You didn't wait for permission to dream—you just did. And even though your voice would sometimes tremble, you still used it.

You had no blueprint. No one in your immediate circle was doing what you wanted to do. But you still chose to believe. You chose to believe that pain could be turned into power. That purpose could be pulled out of your lowest moments. That brokenness didn't disqualify you—it made you relatable. And, Hayls, because of that belief, I now get to live a life I once only imagined.

I remember you joking around in school, saying, 'One day I'm going to speak in Dubai'. People laughed, and even you didn't fully know how or when it would happen—but you *believed*. And now? You don't just speak in Dubai—*you live here*. You walk the streets of a city you once only saw in photos. You sit in boardrooms, host events, and build businesses on soil that once felt impossible.

This wasn't by chance. *This was from decision*. It's because you decided that you would be better, so you could have better. You didn't settle for being a product of your environment. You became a product of your vision.

I know there were moments you felt like quitting. I know there were nights you cried quietly, thinking no one understood. I know you felt pressure to be perfect because people looked up to you, but you were still trying to figure yourself out. I want you to know—you did well. You made mistakes, yes, but *those mistakes were okay*. They didn't cancel your calling. They didn't make you unworthy. In fact, they added depth to your story.

You carried so much at such a young age. And I'm sorry you had to grow up so fast. But please know that everything you went through, every tear, every 'no', every betrayal, every hard lesson—it wasn't wasted. God used *all of it*. Every setback positioned you for a comeback. Every closed door protected you from rooms you weren't called to. Every delay built your character.

Because of your boldness to believe, I can now say I've spoken to over five million people across five continents. That number still blows my mind. From stadiums filled with thousands, to intimate rooms with just a few—your voice has gone global. Because of your resilience, I've scaled businesses across Europe, Africa, and the Middle East. And because of your faith, I'm now mentored by the same man you used to watch on YouTube at 2 a.m.— *Dr Eric Thomas*. Now he mentors you; you've shared the stage with him in London and Atlanta—*and now he's writing your foreword*.

And guess what? You've written not just one but *two books*—and I know there's more to come. You turned your story into strategy. You turned your mess into a message. You turned your wounds into wisdom. And now, your words are sitting on the shelves of people across the world. People you've never met are finding healing in your honesty. That's the power of obedience.

Hayls, you should be so proud of yourself.

Speaking didn't just give me a mic; it gave me a mission. A mission to remind people that their voice matters. That their story matters. That they don't have to have it all together to make an impact. It's opened doors I didn't even know existed. From teaching young girls in Africa the power of affirmation, to spending three months in New York counselling girls from some of the toughest areas in the United States on how to walk in confidence and carry themselves with worth. From sitting with political leaders to praying with broken-hearted teenagers. You've learned how to be both global and grounded, both influential and intentional.

You've flown across continents but never forgotten where you came from. You've built brands and businesses but never traded your values. You've taken the gospel into boardrooms and spoken life into places others said faith didn't belong. You didn't just use your voice to entertain; you used it to *equip*.

You didn't just fight for your future; you fought for mine.

And your fight has freed thousands of young girls to know that it is possible to build without compromise.

You've shown them they *are* good enough, that they *do* belong, and that they don't have to shrink to be seen.

You taught them that softness is not weakness. That boundaries are not bitterness. That you can be powerful *and* peaceful. You taught them that it's okay to say no. That it's okay to cry. That healing is necessary. That those dreams don't die just because things didn't happen on your timeline. You've lived as an example that being set apart is a gift, not a curse.

You've done all this *without ever having to sell out*. And I love you for that. I respect you for that. Because you could have taken shortcuts. You could have compromised. But you didn't. You trusted God. And He trusted you right back.

You've become the woman you needed when you were younger. You've stood in the gap for girls who didn't have the words. You've held space for others while learning how to hold space for yourself. You're not just a speaker. You're a healer. A builder. A light-bearer. A hope-distributor.

So, keep going. Keep speaking. Keep showing up with love, with truth, and with fire. Don't lose your fire just because the platform gets bigger. Don't let the applause distract you from the assignment. Stay anchored. Stay authentic. Stay aligned.

And just remember: the sky is not the limit—*because heaven exists.*

God's got you. He always has.

Mukama Mulungi.

With love,

Mrs Hayley Mulenda Record (age 27 and still dreaming)

Introduction: People Die, Voices Don't

'By silencing your fears, you amplify your voice'.

— Hayley Mulenda

'If you keep quiet at a time like this ... who knows if perhaps you were made queen for such a time as this?'

— Esther 4:14 (NLT)

If life has taught me anything, it's this: many people don't necessarily want to speak, but they deeply wish to be heard.

If you've picked up this book, it means there's something inside you that doesn't just want to speak— you want to be heard. And to be heard, you need to be a voice. What's the difference? Anyone can grab a mic and deliver a few inspirational words, but it takes someone with courage and conviction to be a voice. Being a voice has nothing to do with how well you speak; it has everything to do with how deeply you feel and how tall you'll stand when fighting for something you believe in.

There's a lyric from 'Moment 4 Life' by Nicki Minaj featuring Drake, and he says, 'Everybody dies, but not everybody lives'. I think when you refuse to speak up, and when you refuse to stand for something—when you refuse to be a voice for your values and convictions—you're stripping yourself of the opportunity to really live.

Life is not just about growing old; it's about passing on the stories, lessons, and wisdom to others you'll meet along the way.

One of my favourite fables is *The Alchemist* by Paulo Coelho. It tells the story of a shepherd boy named Santiago who goes on a journey searching for a treasure he saw in a dream. He leaves everything behind and faces hardship, fear, detours, and doubts, but through it all, he learns that the real treasure is never just the gold. The treasure is the transformation, the becoming, the clarity of his voice, and purpose.

Santiago learns what many of us forget: your true purpose isn't something you create out of thin air. It's something you uncover by listening to your inner voice and trusting the process. At one point in the book, Santiago is told, 'When you want something, all the universe conspires in helping you to achieve it'. But that only happens when you move, speak, step out, and stop silencing the internal nudges that have been trying to guide you all along.

Reading that story reminded me that being a voice isn't about finding a mic—it's about finding the courage to follow your calling. Like Santiago, I had to learn that the journey was more about who I was becoming than where I was going.

When I was younger, I would pray to be a booked and busy speaker. Success looked like being booked for back-to-back events, big stages, and big cheques. I started speaking at 15, and back then, I craved the spotlight more than I craved making a difference.

If I'm honest, my motives weren't always pure. I wasn't chasing purpose—I was chasing praise. I found my identity in how people clapped, responded, and saw me. I wanted to be liked, not because I had a message I stood for but because I wanted to be seen.

And that version of me? It reminds me a lot of a man named Saul.

Saul was the first king of Israel. He didn't come from power or prestige. In fact, when he was chosen, he hid— literally. But despite his fear and self-doubt, he was called to lead a nation—to be a voice in his generation.

Saul had everything: the platform, the people, the position—but he got distracted along the way.

He started caring more about what the crowd thought than what he was called to do. He made choices to keep people happy, even when it meant disobeying what was right. His desire to be celebrated by people cost him the very thing he was given: the kingdom. In his need for validation, he lost sight of the bigger picture. He forgot who he was—and, more importantly, who he was meant to be.

And that's the danger. When you live for praise, you lose your place. When you build your life around applause, you slowly silence your own conviction. And if you don't have something deeper anchoring you, you'll drift.

That's why being a voice matters. Not a performer. Not a people-pleaser. A voice. Someone who knows what they stand for—and who they stand for.

The beautiful thing about life is that you can reflect back and rectify particular ways of thinking. I write this book in reflection, as I am no longer 15 and have received everything I prayed for. I have spoken across big stages and stadiums and worked with very big organisations. I have been flown across the world and seen multiple six-figure accounts enter my account because of my voice.

But none of that is what fulfilled me.

What fulfilled me was bumping into a young woman when I was in the shops. She stopped me and said I spoke at her school when she was 16 years old—and now she's 21, about to graduate from university. When she reminded me which school she went to, I remembered it well. The school was in one of the worst boroughs in London. There was high knife crime and a real issue with a lot of girls in her year group getting involved in fraud.

She told me she was on the verge of being excluded—not because she was a bad student, but because it was the norm not to take school seriously. Her focus wasn't on education—it was on being popular. And in her world, being naughty meant she was a pretty well-respected girl in school. But after hearing me speak, she told me she realised that's not how respect works.

Going into her school and being honest, human, and relatable convinced her to think higher than herself and aim for more. She changed her behaviour, put her head down to study, and explained how my example and words made her want to do more with her life and not become a product of her environment.

She's now on a scholarship at a top Russell Group university.

Stories like hers remind me that fulfilment doesn't come from the size of the audience—it comes from the depth of the impact. And I've found that same fulfilment in rooms that look entirely different.

I remember receiving an email from a CEO not too long ago. I delivered a workshop with his leadership team—just an intimate session about communication, authenticity, and the power of connection in leadership. A few days later, he messaged me to say something I'll never forget: 'I've been leading for over a decade, but this is the first time I've felt truly connected to the people I work with every day—because you reminded me to be human and be more vulnerable with my teams'.

He went on to tell me how that one session broke down walls. Team members opened up. Conversations that had been avoided for months finally happened. There was a new sense of unity—less tension, more trust. The culture shifted even slightly, and that shift created a ripple effect in the work environment.

That's the kind of fulfilment that can't be measured in likes, invoices, or applause. It's the quiet reward of knowing your voice, which helped someone believe in their own voice and story again. Whether it's a student in East London or a CEO in a boardroom, being a voice means showing up with purpose and reminding others of the power of their voice, too.

That's what being a voice does. It plants seeds and produces fruit—fruit that others can use to be a voice for change, too.

What Does It Mean to Be a Voice?

Being a voice means your words are more significant than you. It means you're fighting for a cause, for a change, or for something that will outlive you.

Martin Luther King, Jr., was not just a speaker—he was a voice. He didn't just stand on stages; he stood in the face of oppression, declaring, 'I have a dream'. That dream wasn't just his; it was a vision of freedom and equality for millions of people. Because he was a voice, the world shifted. Today, we live in the change he once spoke about.

Mother Teresa wasn't a speaker either—she was a voice. She didn't need microphones or platforms; her actions and words carried the weight of compassion and humility. She fought for the destitute, the forgotten, and the unloved. Her voice reminded the world that every life has value. And even though she's no longer here, her legacy is alive in the thousands of charities, missions, and acts of kindness inspired by her example.

Nelson Mandela was not just a speaker—he was a voice. After 27 years in prison, he could have spoken bitterness, anger, or revenge. Instead, Mandela chose reconciliation. He spoke of unity over a divided South Africa, and because of his voice, apartheid ended, and the seeds of healing were sown. His voice still resonates in a world where justice and equality are battles yet to be fully won.

These people weren't just speakers—they were voices. And here's the truth: People die, but voices don't.

And if there's something else I could highlight about all these individuals, it's their heart to serve. Their voice was to serve others and to contribute to the greater humanity.

Can I be honest?

The Western world can be quite selfish. We are told to manifest and speak about the things we desire— manifest our dreams and manifest our day—but all of this is rooted in self. It's rooted in how we can be blessed rather than in how we can be a blessing to others.

I started feeling so fulfilled when my prayers shifted from 'God, please bless me' to 'God, who can I bless and serve today?' When we allow ourselves to put our ego to the side and serve, that's when we shift to generational impact.

Being a voice starts with two things: an internal conviction and an internal conversation.

The conviction must be rooted in something you live by, stand by, and advocate for. A voice isn't born in comfort—it rises in adversity. Light isn't effective in a room that's already bright; it becomes powerful in darkness. In the same way, a voice rises in times of chaos, injustice, or silence.

Santiago's journey taught me something else; he could've given up at any point. There were moments when fear shouted louder than faith, and comfort looked more appealing than conviction. But had he settled, he would've never discovered who he truly was. His greatest reward wasn't what he found at the end—it was who he became in the process.

And that's what being a voice is all about. It's not about a final destination or stage—it's about becoming someone whose words carry weight because they've been refined by the journey.

It reminds me of another story that's less often quoted but just as powerful.

In the Bible, there's a prophet named Jeremiah. From a young age, he was called, but when God told him to speak to nations, his first response wasn't excitement—it was insecurity. He said, 'I do not know how to speak; I am too young' (Jeremiah 1:6). But God didn't entertain his excuses. Instead, He reminded Jeremiah of one thing: 'Do not be afraid ... for I am with you and will rescue you'.

Jeremiah didn't feel ready. He didn't feel eloquent. He didn't feel seen. But his voice wasn't about his ability—it was about his assignment. And what makes Jeremiah powerful is not just what he said—but how long he stayed faithful to say it. For over 40 years, he prophesied to people who didn't always want to hear the truth. But Jeremiah kept showing up. Because he wasn't performing—he was obeying.

The story of Jeremiah really teaches that your voice may be the only light in a dark place. And it might not change everything, but it will change something—and sometimes, that something is all God needs to start a movement.

This is why I believe the world doesn't need more speakers—it needs more voices rooted in authenticity, integrity, and service.

I really do hope this book sparks an internal conviction in you to become a voice. To stand for something bigger than yourself. To fight for a cause that will outlive you.

But here's the thing: no voice can be expressed externally without first nurturing the inner voice.

Everyone has an internal voice. For some, that voice is critical. For others, it's nurturing. Your internal voice is the foundation for everything you do externally. How can you expect to advocate for others if you don't advocate for yourself? If you don't see yourself as worthy of change, how can you be a voice for change?

I talk about self-sabotage and imposter syndrome more in depth in a later chapter, but you have to learn to nurture an internal voice that charges you and does not deplete you. That internal voice will become your north star and will be the very thing that feeds your conviction.

Martin Luther King, Jr.'s voice for equality was grounded in his internal conviction of faith and justice. Mandela's call for reconciliation came from years of internal dialogue in a prison cell, deciding that unity was more potent than division. Mother Teresa's voice of compassion flowed from an inner well of love and devotion.

And Santiago's voice—though fictional—was a reflection of the very real voice within all of us: the one that longs to live out purpose, to walk with intention, and to trust the process, even when it's unclear.

Everything you do outwardly must be an expression of what you've nurtured inwardly. You cannot pour from an empty cup. You cannot inspire others if you haven't learnt to inspire yourself.

So let me ask you this: what is your internal conviction? What is the cause so deeply rooted in you that you're willing to be a voice for it? Because being a voice means standing for something bigger than you. It means planting seeds of change you may never live to see bloom.

But that's the beauty of being a voice; your words, your actions, and your conviction outlive you.

People die, but voices don't. Be the voice that shifts the atmosphere, that lights up the darkness, and that creates change for generations to come. Be the voice that, long after you're gone, is still speaking.

If there's anything I hope this book inspires in you, it's this: be a voice. Speak with courage. Live with conviction. And stand for something so powerful that your voice will echo for eternity.

PART I

The Psychology Behind Speaking

1

Speaking Is Spiritual

'Death and life are in the power of the tongue'.

— Proverbs 18:21

'Words are free. It's how you use them that may cost you'.

— Rev J Martin

Before we go any further, I need you to understand something: no one else can steward your story like you can. At some point, we all have to stop waiting for someone to hand us a microphone and realise that the power was in our voice all along. Taking personal responsibility doesn't mean blaming yourself for everything that's gone wrong—it means boldly choosing to co-create what comes next. It's easy to repeat the narrative of pain, lack or failure. What's harder—but far more powerful— is realising you have the authority to rewrite the script. You don't have to keep quoting the lies life handed you; you can start scripting the truth. The moment I stopped waiting to be discovered and started declaring who

I already was, things shifted. Personal responsibility is the birthplace of breakthroughs.

I always say that imagination is Heaven's sketchbook. Every bold dream you carry was planted in you for a reason. But imagination without declaration is just a daydream. You've got to give vision vocabulary. One of my favourite stories in the Bible is of Abraham. God told him to look up at the stars and count them—because that's how numerous his descendants would be. God didn't give him a spreadsheet or a strategy first. He gave him a picture. Why? Because the first step to legacy is learning to see what isn't yet there. The second? Speaking as if it already is. I believe imagination is how God invites us to see from His perspective—but what you see must turn into what you say. When imagination meets responsibility, you stop living by default and start living by design.

History is filled with people who didn't just dream loudly—they spoke boldly. Muhammad Ali used to say, 'I am the greatest. I said that even before I knew I was'. That wasn't arrogance—it was alignment. He understood the power of declaring identity before the world recognised it. Jim Carrey, in 1990, wrote himself a $10 million cheque for 'acting services rendered' and dated it for Thanksgiving 1995. He carried it in his wallet as a daily reminder of where he was headed. And almost to the exact year, he landed blockbuster roles in *Ace Ventura*, *The Mask*, and *Dumb and Dumber*, securing the very amount he had once written down in faith. What do people like Ali and Carrey have in common? They understood that words weren't just reflections of desire—they were declarations of destiny. They weren't just speaking about the future—they were calling it forth.

In *The Magic of Thinking Big*, Dr. David J. Schwartz reminds us that success doesn't start with resources but with belief. He writes, 'Believe it can be done. When you believe something can be done, really believe, your mind will find the ways to do it'. The size of your success is determined by the size of your thinking. Small thinking leads to small speaking—and small speaking leads to small living. The innate nature to try and play small is why guarding your thoughts is just as important as guarding your tongue. What lives in your mind will eventually leak through your mouth. If your internal dialogue is limited, your external declarations will be too. Your words are simply the echo of your imagination. And here's the truth: if you can't see it in your mind, you will never release it from your mouth—which means you'll never hold it in your hands.

We have dealt with your thoughts, so now it's time to deal with your words. It's important to understand why your words carry weight. Speaking isn't just about what leaves your mouth; it's about what shapes your future. Something I say often is that speaking is spiritual. There are so many things I am walking in today that I spoke about myself more than 10 years ago.

As I said before, words are spiritual, and words do something. The majority of human beings believe something about themselves or their lives because of something that was said or not said over them.

Now, I will never shy away from the fact that I am a person of faith. I have spent a lot of time in the Bible, and I've realised that the first expression of God is not just God the Creator, but God the Orator. The first exposure of God that we see is of the God who speaks. He says, 'Let there be light', and just like that, light shows up. It's His words that bring order, beauty and life into the world. From the jump, God shows us that words are powerful—and if we're made in His image, what does that say about the power within our own words?

Speaking is spiritual. Every word you say carries weight. Words aren't just sounds; they're seeds, seeds that grow into something. And here's the thing—whether you realise it or not, your words are creating something. The question is: What are they creating? You will either use your words to feed into your destiny or your destruction.

Now, I understand that not everyone may believe in God, so let's look at science—because even science backs this up. Energy is at the core of everything in this world—whether it's a rock, a tree, or you. Energy is made up of waves of vibration. Atoms are constantly moving, constantly vibrating. Now, here's the part that a lot of people forget: when you speak, your words send out vibrations into the world. They're not just ideas; they're actual waves of energy that have an impact on what's around you.

In the early 1990s, Dr Masaru Emoto, a Japanese scientist, conducted an experiment where he studied the impact of words on water. He spoke positive words like 'love' and 'gratitude' over water, and when he froze it, the water formed stunning, intricate crystals. But when he spoke negative words like 'hate' or 'anger', the crystals were chaotic, messy, and broken. Speaking is spiritual—just remember that we're made of over 60% water. If words can literally change the structure of water, think about what your words are doing to you and the people around you.

One of my favourite scriptures says this: Proverbs 18:21: 'Death and life are in the power of the tongue'. I believe in this wholeheartedly. Your words can give life, or they can bring destruction. Think about it: What if God only moved according to the words that came out of your mouth? What if He only acted on what you spoke? Would that make you reconsider your words, and what leaves your mouth?

If there's anything I really want you to take away from this, it's that speaking isn't just about communication, it's about creation. And what you're creating with your words matters.

Scientists have discovered that plants respond to the vibrations of sound, including the words we speak. Researchers at the Indian National Institute of Technology found that certain sound frequencies, including those in human speech, stimulate enzymes in plants that promote growth. This is called plant bioacoustics, and this is a fancy way of saying that plants 'hear' vibrations and respond. When you speak, your words create those vibrations, and plants react by absorbing nutrients more efficiently and growing stronger (Chowdhury et al., 2014). Think about it: your words don't just disappear when they leave your mouth; they ripple outward and influence the world around you.

A study from South Korea, published in *Plant Signaling & Behaviour*, went even further. When plants were exposed to soothing words or sounds, they experienced increased activity in genes related to growth and stress responses. For example, plants exposed to classical music or positive speech developed stronger roots and thrived compared to those exposed to noise or silence (Jeong et al., 2008). Speaking is spiritual; even nature proves it.

If vibrations from words can affect something as simple as a plant, imagine what they can do to a human being. Let's talk about one of the most fascinating pieces of evidence for the power of words: the placebo effect.

In medical research, the placebo effect happens when patients experience real, measurable improvements simply because they believe in the treatment—even when it's just a sugar pill. The key? Words of assurance and belief. In a study published in *The Lancet*, patients who were told by their doctor, 'This treatment will help you', experienced significant pain relief—even though the treatment was a placebo. Brain scans showed that the verbal suggestion activated the brain's natural opioid pathways, which reduced pain (Benedetti et al., 2005).

This isn't just psychology; it's biology. Words spoken with belief and intention trigger responses in the brain and body that align with what was spoken. Another study in *Science Translational Medicine* found that even when patients unknowingly received placebos, their bodies responded positively when healthcare providers spoke with confidence and reassurance (Kaptchuk et al., 2008). The spoken word literally shaped their healing process.

Let's bring this back to you. If words can stimulate plants to grow and trick the human brain into activating healing pathways, how much more could your words influence your own growth—or even your own healing? Remember, words are not just sounds; they are vibrations, energy, and tools of creation. When you speak over your life—whether positively or negatively—you're planting seeds.

Here's what I want you to think about: Are your words building or breaking? Are you speaking life, or are you sowing seeds of doubt, fear, and negativity? Because whether you realise it or not, you're shaping your reality—and the realities of others—with every word you say. Speaking is spiritual because it's a reflection of who we are and whose we are.

God spoke light into the darkness. Now, He's given you that same power in your voice. So, what are you going to do with it?

When I understood how much power was in my words, I didn't just become intentional—I became directional. I have been speaking since the age of 15, and I didn't have any plans. All I had was hope, vision, and determination. I'll be real—I didn't even know that I could build a career in public speaking, but I knew there was something within me that wanted to use my voice to speak into people's destinies, not their destruction.

From a young age, I have always used my words to uplift others. I remember coming across a video in 2012 of Dr Eric Thomas talking about how he came from poverty and became the number one motivational speaker in the world. He didn't make excuses; he focused on becoming the best version of himself. That video gave me goosebumps. I just knew I wanted to make people feel the same way he made me feel.

So I started looking for ways to do that. In 2012, I decided to run for Young Mayor of Newham. I wanted to advocate for young people in my area. I grew up in one of the poorest areas in London—Newham. I believed that young people in Newham needed better representation, so I started my campaign by rallying a group of young people across my school. I built my campaign team to over 60 teenagers aged 15 and 16, speaking life into them, empowering them, and telling them they were part of a bigger picture and a bigger change for Newham.

At the time, Newham had gone through a lot of gentrification—this was the same year London was hosting the Olympics, and guess what area was hosting it? Newham. I didn't think it was fair that the area would improve, but the young people wouldn't. I would actively speak life into my team to motivate and inspire them. My words were making a change. My words were empowering them to want to change Newham.

The words couldn't be seen, but they could be felt. The words that matter are felt. Words are spiritual, and there's no denying that.

Even though I didn't win the campaign, I came third out of 54 candidates, with over 900 votes across the Newham borough. Even though I lost the campaign, I gained a revelation, and that revelation was that words are spiritual. And that revelation changed everything for me.

In 2009/2010, I faced severe bullying, and that experience completely knocked my confidence. Not only was I scared to speak up, but I was completely scared of leaving my house. The bubbly, confident Hayley had now become a shell of herself, silent and withdrawn. The bullying continued for three years. The girls in my year group went on to hack my Myspace and Facebook accounts and spread rumours. These rumours weren't just about my appearance; they attacked my character. I genuinely felt like the whole world was against me. I would never wish that experience on anyone.

I remember hearing this rhyme growing up: 'Sticks and stones may break my bones, but words will never hurt me'. But the reality is, those words didn't just hurt me. They broke me. They festered in my spirit until I no longer felt good enough. I didn't think I was pretty enough. My self-esteem was crushed, and I lived with those beliefs for years.

You know, every single one of us carries a limiting belief about ourselves because of words that were spoken or words that weren't spoken over us. And that experience planted something in me. It made me want to use my voice to empower others. Being someone who was made to feel like crap, I didn't want anyone else to feel that way. That's one of the reasons I decided to run for Young Mayor of Newham. I knew what it was like to be silenced and overlooked—and I wanted to be a voice for those who felt the same.

As much as I wanted to speak life into others, I had to learn to speak life into myself first. I realised that if I was going to help others believe in their value, I had to start by believing in mine. I couldn't keep pouring encouragement into others while starving myself of the same truth. Speaking wasn't just about motivating the world around me—it became about healing the world within me. That's when things shifted. I started speaking over my life, over my future, and over my purpose.

At the age of 15, I didn't just say I wanted to be a speaker; I said I wanted to be a world-renowned international speaker. My friend Freditta once said that I always spoke in the superlative, always using the most gigantic words to describe something or someone. How could I use those words about everything and everyone else, but not say them about myself?

In my early speaking career, I wrote out a dream biography: 'Hayley Mulenda is a multi-award-winning international speaker, impacting millions across the globe and working with some of the world's most influential leaders and organisations'. Can you imagine the same biography I wrote at 15 is the same biography the MCs read about me now, 12 years later! it's not fiction; it's for real.

I remember buying myself a map at 18. I hadn't been booked for any international speaking engagements yet, but I was sure I would be international one day. I'd look at the map and say, 'USA, HAYLEY IS COMING SOON', 'DUBAI, HAYLEY IS COMING SOON', 'GHANA, HAYLEY IS COMING SOON'. I spoke those words over so many nations. And guess what? Every nation my 18-year-old self-spoke about—I now have multiple clients in. The United States, the Middle East, Africa, and Europe—all of it became reality because of the faith of a little 15-year-old girl from East London.

Looking back, I realise now that I wasn't just speaking over my future; I was partnering with it. Every declaration I made at 15 wasn't random—it was spiritual. I was sowing words like seeds, and I've been living in the harvest ever since. The bio I wrote at 15 is the one being read at global events. The map I prayed over is now filled with clients. And the mentor I once dreamed of having is now writing the foreword to this very book. That's not a coincidence—that's alignment. That's what happens when you take your words seriously. So, if there's anything I've learned, it's this: don't speak based on where you are—speak based on where you're going. Your words are setting the stage before your feet ever arrive. Speaking is spiritual. So speak with faith, speak with vision, and speak with the boldness of someone who knows Heaven is listening.

If this whole chapter were to be summarised into a framework, this would be it: The S.P.E.A.K. Framework.

If speaking is spiritual, then here are a few important things to remember.

- *S—See it before you say it. Let imagination sketch what's possible.*

- *P—Proclaim it with faith. Speak about what hasn't happened yet as if it has.*

- *E—Eliminate the thoughts that shrink you.*

- *A—Affirm your identity daily. Words shape belief. Belief shapes destiny.*

- *K—Kindle others with your voice. Your words should ignite—not just impress.*

Speak life. Speak vision. Speak up.

Journaling Prompt

What is one vision for your future that you're ready to start speaking out loud again? Please write it down as a declaration, and read it over yourself every day for the next seven days.

2

Real Models over Role Models

'Integrity is doing the right thing, even when no one is watching'.

— C.S. LEWIS

'People look at the outward appearance, but the Lord looks at the heart'.

— 1 Samuel 16:7 (NIV)

If words build worlds, then character holds them together. It's one thing to speak powerfully, but it's another to live truthfully. In a time when everyone's trying to be seen, what sets you apart isn't just your message—it's your integrity. People don't just listen to what you say—they watch how you live. And more than a role model, what this world needs is a real model. Someone whose life speaks louder than their platform.

We live in a world where we have many influencers but not many examples. In 2016, there was a shift in culture, and that shift was the rise of influencers. In the days of my childhood, campaigns would use celebrity voices to push a product/message or campaign. However, the rise of YouTube shifted who we deemed as influential and who we actually wanted to hear from. We started to see people wanting to engage with the everyday person who took a chance on themselves to create content. Celebrities now had to adapt and include organic content in their campaigns quickly. Influencer marketing changed everything.

The rise of influencers changed how people engage with content and how people create content. I remember reading a book called *The 21 Irrefutable Laws of Leadership* by John C. Maxwell—this book highlights the importance of leadership and not settling for a title. It also emphasises that a title is the lowest level of leadership. You cannot lead people with words; you must lead with integrity. The rise of social media has fed people the desire to be an influencer rather than to be influential. Being an influencer feeds into the false narrative of perfectionism, and that can be very dangerous. Many are trying to be role models, but the secret to standing out is being a real model. Being real is always ideal.

Integrity means to be integrated, it means to be one and to be whole—unfortunately, many people live separate from their core message, their words do not reflect their life and their life does not reflect their words.

As human beings, we are sometimes scared of truly being seen. We are living in a time where the word 'perfectionist' is used subconsciously by many people to describe themselves. I believe that many people have a minor trait of perfectionism due to the digital age in which we live. Dr Brené Brown once stated, 'Perfectionism doesn't protect you from judgement; it protects you from being seen'.

I believe that in modern society, social media and Web 2.0 have shaped the way we view ourselves, and many people now compare themselves to someone's perfect Instagram picture, the life they see on someone's Facebook page, or the new ventures/milestones they may see others post on their LinkedIn profile. Many have fallen into the trap of proving themselves by posting all the good but not the real. It feeds into a pressure that makes many speak about a life they do not have and pretend to have a lifestyle they cannot attain.

Social media feeds into a microwave era, that success comes quickly and that it can happen overnight. Even though a microwave heats food and can cook food, a microwave can never cook your food at the same quality as an oven.

An oven makes sure the food is cooked thoroughly; even though the process is longer, the process is more efficient. What makes your message worth listening to is the process. Words have nothing to do with how they sound; they have everything to do with how they feel. The depth of your message is determined by the depth of your process.

In a time where being a personality can make you a global sensation—people feel standing out is no longer down to depth; it's down to views, and that is a LIE. Your skills, views, and competence will get you into the room, but it's your character, personality, and authenticity that will keep you there. Where imposter syndrome is at an all-time high, many question whether competence is essential. Competence will always be necessary, but integrity conquers all.

As someone who has been networking from the age of 16, I sometimes found it hard to connect with certain individuals. It's only now that I realise that it had nothing to do with what they were doing; it had everything to do with the fact that I didn't feel they were genuine. The power of integrity is rooted in our honesty, not with others but with ourselves. When we are authentic, we are more likely to be perceived as genuine and trustworthy.

When you walk in integrity, you are less likely to experience inner conflict or doubt because you are living in alignment with your true selves.

It's very likely that if you are clothed in shame and guilt, you'll find it hard to be genuine with others, because you're not even being genuine with yourself.

Authenticity starts with self-awareness. We sometimes have to have an honest conversation about our traumas, triggers, life lessons, and past pain points. We have to learn to be honest about our strengths and our weaknesses.

My husband once told me, 'Don't let criticism get to your heart and don't let compliments get to your head'. Compliments can feed into your ego, and criticism can feed into your insecurities. We need to learn to handle both in a healthy way, and that starts with us dealing with it directly first.

It's easy to point fingers and point out where others are strong or where others need to do the work, but we need to learn to regularly engage in conversations within our soul that help identify areas for improvement, areas we need to heal, and areas we need to celebrate more.

I know that being transparent is not always easy, especially in a time where it's very easy to fake it till you make it, but what does it profit a man to gain the world but lose his soul? If I am to refer to the Bible, when God created the earth, Genesis 2:25 talks about how God made us naked and unashamed. I know that everyone can have their own interpretations and outlooks on that verse, but for me, I take away the idea that God created us to be transparent and real.

No connection can thrive from inauthenticity. Every genuine connection must be rooted in truth. It must be rooted in transparency, but as Michael Jackson once said, 'It starts with the man in the mirror'.

Integrity helps us build stronger relationships, stronger brands, strong presence, and stronger messages. Integrity will help you find clarity and purpose, and achieve personal growth and fulfilment. It is the one asset that we can all cultivate in our lives, and it is a quality that has a positive impact on our well-being and success.

As humans, we are more critical of ourselves than of others. Sometimes, we can convince ourselves to pursue perfection rather than pursue transparency. My vulnerability has been the key for me to step into many rooms—rooms that I probably was not qualified for and rooms that I was told would never want a girl like me in. I am a young Black female who grew up in a single-parent household in East London; what makes me special? Nothing. But what makes me stand out? I choose to be myself.

An old mentor of mine told me CEOs and corporate executives wouldn't want to hear from me because I am a young Black woman who speaks slang, but the same corporations he told me would not want to hear from me are the same corporations I have had the opportunity to consult for—helping them engage with their Gen Z diverse talent and helping consult on their inclusion policies—and overview their impact work for social mobility.

Integrity allows you to do the work you love with no compromise.

One of my favourite quotes will always be 'The truth will set you free'. Being myself has been the most freeing experience, and as I have had the opportunity to connect with top CEOs and leaders around the world, I have seen that the older you get, the more perfect you tell yourself to be. I have always wondered why children seem to overcome negative emotions quickly, and why they have more determination. I figured it was simply because their minds are blank canvases. They have not yet grasped perfectionism; this doesn't exist in their world unless someone tells them otherwise.

The world has told us a lie; they told us we have to be one way to be successful. There are so many self-help books that will outline many different principles for you to implement in your life; most of those principles are low-key telling you, 'You're not good enough, and you need to change'. I hate the idea of trying to change who you are without first discovering or embracing who you are.

This now means you feel the pressure to live a life which is not true to you.

If there's anything my journey has taught me, it is that a microphone amplifies your voice, but authenticity is what will amplify your message.

When I think about the greatest speakers in history, it's not just their words that they're remembered for; it's how they carried themselves and how they lived their lives. We are human beings, not human doings—which means everything you do must be rooted in the very essence of who you are. We need to shift from performing to being. In our current world, it is very easy to build a life of performance. You can post a life that does not really exist. I sometimes think about the fact that it's called Instagram stories. It's because Instagram stories get to tell your followers a story; the story doesn't necessarily have to be true. We have many people who are telling stories that they're not actually living, and that is a very dangerous place to be.

Would you ever respect the charismatic speaker who rallies crowds about family values but neglects their own children? Society often separates 'the message' from 'the human', but you just can't. People will always smell when someone isn't themselves. People will always sense dissonance. When your private life contradicts your public words, you don't just lose credibility—you betray the very message you claim to stand by.

How can you expect others to believe your words if you don't believe them enough to live by them?

Mid-chapter reflection: When was the last time you felt the pressure to perform instead of just show up as you?

Authenticity isn't just a buzzword. It's the alignment of your truth, lived out truthfully in your actions, values, and words, especially when no one's watching. Consider it the root system of a tree: Hidden, but the reason the tree stands tall. Or consider it to be like electricity; it empowers everything around you—even though it remains unseen.

When I first started speaking, I wanted to sound like Eric Thomas. He inspired me so much that I'd go around school literally shouting at students, thinking that kind of intensity was what made someone powerful. I thought if I could speak like E.T., maybe I'd be successful like him. But I didn't realise then that trying to imitate someone else was costing me my own voice.

One of my earliest mentors, Action Jackson, was the first person who helped me believe that speaking wasn't just a passion—it could be a profession. He inspired me to start speaking too—outside of people like Eric Thomas, whom I had always looked up to. I'll never forget what Jackson told me when I was around 18. He sat me down one day and said, 'Hayley, you actually speak better when you're softer. You're a powerful speaker, but there's something about your softness that shifts the room. You don't have to sound like E.T. You sound great just the way you are'.

That conversation anchored something in me.

It was the first time I realised that my power wasn't in my performance—it was in my presence. That my voice didn't need to be loud to be heard. That my softness wasn't a setback; it was my secret weapon. I'll share more about how Jackson became such an important part of my journey in the next chapter—but just know, that moment freed me. It gave me permission to be me.

We need to stop trying to be perfect; perfection doesn't exist. Just focus on being honest. Share your struggles, your triumphs. It's your struggles that make you human.

In 2020, I came across a DJ called DJ D-Sol. I started reading his profile and was impressed by his credentials. But what truly caught my attention was discovering that DJ D-Sol was actually David Solomon, the CEO of Goldman Sachs. Here was a man leading one of the most powerful financial institutions in the world, yet still finding time to be in the booth, pursuing a passion that grounded him. That challenged me, because for so long,

I believed that certain parts of me had to stay hidden in order to be taken seriously. But seeing him live fully in both lanes gave me permission to *reclaim mine*.

It made me realise that sometimes, we don't need a rebrand—we need to return to the parts of ourselves we abandoned to be accepted.

I've been singing since the age of four, and rapping since I was eight. But somewhere along the line, I let fear tell me that music didn't 'fit' the brand I had built as a speaker. I boxed my creativity for the sake of control. I silenced my sound because I didn't want to confuse the audience I worked so hard to build.

Then COVID hit. The world paused, and so did the performance. I started asking myself deeper questions about my joy. *When was the last time I did something purely because it made me come alive? So,* I went back to the basics. I went to the thing that brought me joy as a child. Believe it or not, it was rapping. I found Beats on YouTube. I started writing again, and rapping again. This was feeding my inner child. A lot of adults have grown up neglecting the things that bring them joy, the hobbies they once participated in that gave them drive and made them feel alive. I believe it's because most people fall into the trap of having responsibilities, and then neglecting their hobbies. I decided that I couldn't fall into the same trap. I needed a hobby, and I needed a life.

So while building my speaking career, I pursued music. I released songs. I performed at the BBC Roundhouse in

Chalk Farm. I reached the *top three* in the UK iTunes Rap chart on my release day. Even though I was pursuing music, many artists get lost in the stats; for me, it wasn't about the numbers; it was actually about the narrative. I reclaimed my voice, not just as a speaker, but as a storyteller. And the moment I did that, opportunities opened. Not because I became someone new, but because I finally gave myself permission to be *me*. There's a scripture that says, 'The fear of man is a snare' (Proverbs 29:25), and I know what it feels like to be trapped by perception. It's limiting. I may not be *everyone's idea of perfect, but I'm true*.

Being a real model isn't about being flawless; it's about being *faithful* to who you are.

One of the turning points for me was living in the contrast. I'd be flying out to speak to executives and CEOs, and then catching the bus back to the ends. I wanted to tell that story, not edit it. So, I wrote a song called 'Prosper'. This is the part of the book where you find out that I am a rapper. The chorus says, 'Sometimes I eat Dixy, and sometimes I eat lobster'. We shot the music video between an office and a council estate because both were my reality. One day, I would be in boardrooms; the next, I'd be walking through my council estate in my Canada Goose. And I no longer see that tension as something to fix—I see it as something to *feature*.

For a long time, I thought my background disqualified me. I used to feel shame about being raised in a single-parent household in a rough area. But music helped me articulate my story in a way that reached the very people I'm called to. It gave me another mic, another platform, another chance to show up for those who may never step into a conference room but might just be lovers of rap music.

I never realised this until my mid-20s, but now I know that my upbringing was not my limitation; if anything, it was a ladder. I convinced myself for years to hide where I am from and to project it like I had it all together. I would shy away from the truth and become trapped by perfection, but the truth is, the world doesn't need another perfect profile—it needs more *real people*. People who are consistent in private, not just curated in public. We need people who live lives that match their message. Your influence doesn't begin on a platform— it begins in the mirror. The more you embrace who you are, the more space you give others to do the same. Being a real model is not about being flawless; it's about being *faithful* to the truth of who you are. Not everyone will get it, but the right people—the ones assigned to your voice, message, and mission—*will*. And you'll realise that the very thing you were tempted to hide was the thing God wanted to *highlight*.

Where in your life have you been performing instead of being? What's one area where you can start showing up more truthfully, even if it's uncomfortable?

Real models don't just inspire with their words— they influence with their walk. So before you try to be followed, be someone worth following. Because your greatest legacy won't come from how many people clapped for you—but how many people were changed because you were real.

Journaling Prompt

Where in your life are you performing instead of showing up as your real self—and what would it look like to lead from that place instead?

3

You Are Not an Imposter

'You can be the most qualified person in the room and still feel like you don't belong. That doesn't make you a fraud. That makes you human'.

— Michelle Obama

'But he said to me, "My grace is sufficient for you, for my power is made perfect in weakness." Therefore I will boast all the more gladly about my weaknesses, so that Christ's power may rest on me'.

— 2 Corinthians 12:9 (NIV)

When you commit to being real, you'll quickly discover how loud the lies can get. The moment you stop performing and start showing up as yourself, imposter syndrome often creeps in, making you question whether you're enough, belong, or are just pretending after all. It's one thing to decide to live authentically. It's another thing to silence the voice that tells you authenticity isn't enough. Being a real model doesn't mean you won't battle insecurity—it just means you've chosen not to let it lead you.

Studies show that up to 70% of people will experience imposter syndrome at some point (Clance & Imes, 1978; Sakulku, J., & Alexander, J., 2011). But let's be honest—when it shows up, it doesn't feel like a stat. It feels personal. Doubt doesn't check your resume—it checks your *confidence*. It doesn't matter how talented, qualified, or experienced you are. Imposter syndrome creeps in quietly and questions everything loudly.

Take someone like Sarah—a senior consultant in her late 30s. On paper, she was thriving: respected by her peers, leading big projects, and earning well. But inside? She felt like a fraud. Every win was credited to luck. Every compliment was dismissed. She was constantly waiting for someone to 'find her out'. The anxiety affected her sleep, her joy, and even how she showed up in relationships. And the worst part? No one could tell. Because imposter syndrome doesn't always look like panic—it often looks like perfection.

Imposter syndrome doesn't discriminate. It doesn't matter how talented, loved, or successful you are. Even some of the most recognisable actors—people with Oscars, global fan bases, and decades of experience—have confessed to moments where they felt like they didn't belong.

Tom Hanks, for example, once admitted:

'No matter what we've done, there comes a point where you think, "How did I get here? When are they going to discover that I am, in fact, a fraud and take everything away from me?"'

Emma Watson, after the Harry Potter series, shared:

'It's almost like the better I do, the more my feeling of inadequacy increases. I've wrestled a lot with the belief that I don't deserve to be here'.

And then there's Will Smith—someone many of us grew up watching on screen. In one of the most iconic episodes of *The Fresh Prince of Bel-Air*, there's a moment where Will's character breaks down in front of Uncle Phil after his on-screen dad walks out on him. The line 'How come he don't want me, man?' shattered hearts worldwide.

In a later interview, Will revealed that those were real tears. That moment wasn't acting—it was *his* pain, bleeding through the script. Because he didn't have the best relationship with his father in real life, that scene triggered something deep, and the emotion you saw was raw, unscripted, and deeply personal.

Imposter syndrome could have silenced that story. It could've convinced him to hold back, to keep it polished, to 'stay in character'. But instead, he chose to be present. And that vulnerability made the scene unforgettable— for him and millions who saw themselves in it. That's the power of showing up fully. That's what happens when you stop pretending and start being *real*.

I was just 15 years old when I faced imposter syndrome for the first time. I had decided to run for Young Mayor in my borough, and part of the campaign meant standing in front of my entire school to deliver an assembly.

I stood backstage, gripping my notes, whispering prayers under my breath. My heart was racing, my hands were shaking, and my thoughts were spiralling. *What if they laugh? What if no one votes? What if I sound stupid? What if I'm not enough?*

I'm not good enough.

At least, that's what I told myself—and worse, I believed it.

Growing up in a low socio-economic background, I wasn't the most articulate. I spoke with a lot of slang, and I didn't always pronounce my T's properly. I remember when I was first starting out in speaking, I had someone I looked up to as a mentor. They said to me that 'I wasn't articulate enough. No one would want to hear someone like me speak'—this led to quite a lot of insecurity with how I articulate myself, and it led to me subconsciously comparing myself to others who seemed so much more polished. I felt like an imposter in my early days of speaking—who would want to listen to a young girl who speaks slang and does not pronounce her words properly?

But here's the thing about imposter syndrome: it doesn't care about your potential. It doesn't care about your dreams. It only cares about keeping you small, safe, and stuck. And for a long time, I let it win. I let it convince me that I wasn't ready, that I didn't deserve to be heard, that I should wait until I was 'perfect' before I allowed myself to reach out for particular opportunities.

I said it in the previous chapter, and I will repeat it: perfection doesn't exist.

I want to give you a background into the type of upbringing I had—I grew up on a channel called Channel U. It was the grime era, where everyone gathered into Charlie's Booth, talking about how they want to make it out the ends, and the ends made them heartless. I never understood the weight of their storytelling until I was older, and I could relate.

I have a big heart, and I am actually quite a sensitive individual, but if you want to survive, my characteristics make me the weakest link, so I had to lie to myself that being heartless was the way forward.

From a young age, I started to develop a tough girl persona, which led to me fighting. The best way to earn respect was to be someone who could fight. I grew up watching World Wrestling Entertainment (WWE), and I had an older brother who used to play rough with me; he made me get into fighting, WWE, Grime, and Rap— My older brother has always been a hero to me; he was the only male voice I had in my life at the time. My unhealed daddy issues made me want to do everything he wanted. I aspired to make him proud, so I started telling myself to be more like him and less like myself.

I spent a lot of my childhood growing up around boys and fighting boys—I remember when I was around eight years old, and I got into a fight with another kid at my aunt's house. I practised the moves I learned from WWE and ended up knocking out the boy's front two teeth—he started crying, and everyone cheered me on and started stating that I was cool.

I think it's at that moment that I started to be attentive to what people think about me. I not only wanted to be popular, but I wanted to be respected, and in my head, being heartless was what made you respected. Even though I went to a Catholic school, I found myself listening to music that had severe profanity, and that brought me joy. Growing up in a strict African household meant that I grew up in a lot of secrecy.

I watched my 18+ rated music videos while my mum was at work; I would chant around the house, swearing at the top of my lungs, but not too loud because I didn't want my brother to hear me. I would go to my aunt's house and start fighting boys, and I always made sure my mum was to never find out.

I kind of liked the idea of living a double life. I wanted to come across as the driven, innocent, ambitious angel for my mum, and the heartless, tough kid who doesn't take BS to the others.

At 15years old, I had a knife drawn on me for my BlackBerry; it was one of my friends who had set me up. He needed the money, and I was the perfect target; as I said, in the end, you have to be heartless.

It didn't matter that this was the same boy who I used to play out with—at this point, that didn't matter. I had known my friend for a few years; we used to play out when I was around 11 years old. We often spoke on BBM (BlackBerry Messenger), and he introduced me to a few gang bangers in the end. So when he texted me saying he wanted to meet in West Ham Park to buy a BlackBerry, the last thing that was running through my mind was that he was going to try and get me stabbed. He said he would be there to meet me, and it'd be good to catch up. I knew he was on the roads, and I knew he was dabbling in gang culture, but I thought to myself, 'he wouldn't hurt me; we go way back' but I have to give context—even though he was my friend, he was actually from the opp side (which means he was from the rival area where I had grown up).

As I said, I wanted respect—even if it meant getting respect from boys who should be 'opps', then so be it. I wasn't ever involved in gang culture, but growing up in the ends kind of throws you in the middle of it if you're not careful.

I remember sitting on a bench in West Ham Park and messaging him on BBM, saying that I was there and that I was waiting for him.

Next thing I knew, a tall boy walked up to me with a Bally (balaclava) on his face, and he said give me your phone while holding a knife to me. He was just about to press the knife into my abdomen, but I started screaming for help as soon as I saw the knife. A bystander immediately called the police. A woman who was on a jog saw what was happening, and she ran over to me and shouted, 'OI, WHAT YOU DOING TO HER?'

She comforted me until the police came. The police asked me to go with them; I told them I couldn't do that, and as soon as they turned their back to speak to the bystander, I ran away.

I ran away because 'snitches get stitches', and I am not a snitch. I remember that after running around the corner and crying, I had the realisation that I could've easily become a statistic. 'Young female stabbed to death in East London' is what the headline would've been to describe me. As I was running away from the police, I remember stopping at a corner and crying, thinking, 'How would they tell my mum? What would my brother do? Would I be a memorial in my secondary school?' So many thoughts ran through my head at this point, and one of those thoughts was 'I need to make it out of here; this can't be my life'.

Growing up in the ends is not just a phrase; it's real life. I remember watching the news as they announced another young person had died on TV because of a knife crime. I would remember myself saying, 'Wow, that's sad'—as time went on, I started to recognise some of the young people on my TV screen; a few times, I recognised friends, and unfortunately, in 2018, it happened to be my own cousin who was stabbed to death.

So now that I am in a place where I want to start using my voice for something positive, even though being around a lot of trauma, I have a lot of odds set up against me. My background made me feel I was a product of my environment, and that's all I would ever be—a girl from the ends, stuck in a cycle/system of trauma.

It took me years to realise that my voice mattered. I grew up in an environment where speaking up could get you into trouble with gang affiliation or the law. However, my perspective, my story, my struggles, and my triumphs were all pieces of a puzzle that only I could share. The same is true for you.

Imposter syndrome thrives on lies. It tells us we're not smart enough, not talented enough, not experienced enough. It convinces us that we're frauds, that we've somehow tricked people into believing in us, and that we'll be exposed sooner or later.

For me, those lies sounded like this:

> You're too young to be taken seriously.
> You're not articulate enough to inspire anyone.
> You don't have anything valuable to say.

Sound familiar? Maybe your lies are different, but they all stem from the same place: fear. Fear of failure. Fear of judgement. Fear of not being enough.

A study was conducted with people who were terminally ill to determine their biggest regrets. Every one of those who answered the question shared that their biggest regret was caring too much about what people think. I often wonder how many people hold back from speaking up because the opinions of others have snared them.

Do you know what I have found: those opinions only have power if you allow them to.

I was bullied in my early years of secondary school, so having that experience on top of everything else really impacted me. I was a prisoner of other people's opinions. At one point, I tried being the class clown because I so badly wanted to impress others that I didn't even realise I was imprisoned by other people's opinions of me, which fed more into my imposter syndrome.

My journey to overcoming imposter syndrome didn't happen overnight. It was a series of small, courageous steps that eventually led to a breakthrough. One of those steps was my first speaking engagement at 15.

I remember walking onto that stage, my legs trembling, my voice shaking. I felt like an imposter, like I didn't belong. But as I started speaking, something shifted. I looked out into the audience and saw some faces nodding, and people connecting with my words. At that moment, I realised something profound: my voice had power. Not because I was perfect, but because I was authentic.

That experience taught me a valuable lesson: confidence isn't something you're born with—it's something you build. And the only way to build it is by taking a chance on yourself before expecting anyone else to.

One of the biggest obstacles I faced was my own limiting beliefs. These were the stories I had internalised over the years that told me I wasn't good enough, smart enough, or worthy enough.

Here are some of the limiting beliefs I had to confront:

'I'm too young to be taken seriously'.

The truth: Age is just a number. Wisdom and insight aren't determined by how many years you've lived, but by the experiences and lessons you've learned. I often learn from those younger than me.

'I'm not articulate enough'.

The truth: Articulation isn't about using big words or speaking flawlessly. It's about communicating with clarity, passion, and authenticity.

'I don't have anything valuable to say'.

The truth: Your story is unique, and your perspective matters. What you have to say could be exactly what someone else needs to hear.

Breaking free from these beliefs wasn't easy. It required me to challenge my thoughts, question the narratives I had been telling myself, and replace them with empowering truths.

One of the most powerful tools I discovered on my journey was speaking life into yourself. The voice you will hear 24/7 is actually yours, so you might as well make it kind to yourself.

I started speaking to myself with more kindness and encouragement.

Here are some of the affirmations I used to rewire my mindset:

I am wonderfully and fearfully made.

My voice matters, and my story has value.

God brought me into this world, which means my voice is necessary.

These affirmations became my anchor, reminding me of my worth, even when self-doubt tried to creep in.

I didn't overcome imposter syndrome on my own. Along the way, I was fortunate to have mentors and a supportive community who believed in me, even when I didn't believe in myself.

In the previous chapter, I mentioned Jackson Ogunyemi, aka Action Jackson. I can't ever share my speaking story and not bring him up. Jackson came to speak at my primary school when I was 10 years old. It was such an assembly, and that planted the seed for me. I didn't see Jackson again until I was 16 years old, my first week of sixth form.

He did such a fantastic assembly, and I looked at him and desired to do what he was doing. He then called different students up to the stage and asked them what they wanted to do; my friends forced me to go onto the stage and share. He came to me and asked me what I wanted to do, and I responded by saying, 'I want to do what you do, but better' (*this is the class clown creeping in, haha*). He took a step back, chuckled, and said. 'Yeah, I need to mentor you'.

He knew there was something in me that needed to be unlocked. Mentorship unlocks potential and makes it your reality, something he told me in my early years of being mentored by him: 'You don't have to be great to start, but you have to start to be great'. Those words stuck with me, reminding me that growth happens when you intentionally break out of your comfort zone.

If you're struggling with imposter syndrome, I encourage you to seek out mentors and communities that uplift and inspire you. Surround yourself with people who see your potential, even when you can't see it yourself.

One of the most insidious effects of imposter syndrome is self-sabotage. It's that voice that tells you to turn down opportunities, to play small, to stay in the background where it's safe.

I've been there. I've talked myself out of opportunities because I didn't think I was good enough. I've let fear dictate my decisions, only to regret it later.

But here's what I've learned: every time you say no to an opportunity because of fear, you're saying no to your own growth. You're denying yourself the chance to learn, grow, and prove that you're capable of more than you think.

If you're ready to break free from imposter syndrome and step into your power, here are some actionable steps you can take:

The first step to overcoming imposter syndrome is to recognise it. Name, acknowledge, and remind yourself that it's a common experience.

Write down the beliefs that are holding you back. Then, challenge them with evidence to the contrary. For example, if you believe you're not good enough, list your accomplishments, and the people who believe in you.

Reframe Failure

Instead of seeing failure as proof of your inadequacy, see it as an opportunity to learn and grow. Every mistake is a stepping stone to success.

Celebrate Your Wins

Take time to celebrate your achievements, no matter how small. Acknowledging your progress will help you build confidence, and silence your inner critic.

Take Action

The best way to overcome imposter syndrome is to take action. Say yes to opportunities, even when you're scared. Each step you take will prove to yourself that you're capable of more than you think.

Your Voice Matters

Looking back, I'm grateful for the journey that brought me here. Every stumble, moment of self-doubt, and time I pushed through fear led me to where I am today.

And now, I want to remind you that your voice matters. Your story matters. You don't have to be perfect to make an impact. You just have to be brave enough to show up, speak up, and share your truth.

One of the most beautiful things about overcoming imposter syndrome is the ripple effect it creates. You permit others to do the same when you step into your power, and share your story.

I remember watching Coach Carter and coming across this poem.

Our deepest fear is not that we are inadequate.

Our deepest fear is that we are powerful beyond measure.

It is our light, not our darkness, that most frightens us.

We ask ourselves, 'Who am I to be brilliant, gorgeous, talented, fabulous?'

Actually, who are you not to be?

You are a child of God.

Your playing small does not serve the world.

There is nothing enlightened about shrinking so that other people won't feel insecure around you.

We are all meant to shine, as children do.

We were born to manifest the glory of God within us.

It's not just in some of us; it's in everyone.

And as we let our own light shine, we unconsciously give other people permission to do the same.

Our presence automatically liberates others as we are liberated from our fear.

I recite this every day as a reminder to myself that stepping into my light gives other people the power to do the same.

I'll never forget when a young girl approached me after my talks. She was shy, her voice barely above a whisper, but her eyes were filled with determination. 'I want to be a speaker too', she said, 'but I don't think I'm good enough'.

Hearing those words felt like looking into a mirror. I saw myself in her—the fear, the self-doubt, the longing to be seen and heard. And in that moment, I realised that my journey wasn't just about me. It was about showing others that they could do it, too.

So, I told her what I wish someone had told me at 16: 'You don't have to be perfect. You just have to be brave'.

So I challenge you: what limiting beliefs are holding you back? What opportunities have you talked yourself out of because of fear? What would happen if you took one small step towards your dreams today?

Remember, you don't have to have it all figured out to start, and that's okay.

Imposter syndrome may never entirely go away, but it doesn't have to control you. Every time you choose courage over fear, and action over self-doubt, you're proving to yourself that you're capable of more than you think.

You are enough. You are worthy. And you have something valuable to offer the world.

So take a deep breath, step into the spotlight, and let your voice be heard. The world is waiting for you.

As you reflect on your own journey, I want to leave you with a challenge. Think about one area of your life where imposter syndrome is holding you back. Maybe it's your career, your relationships, or a dream you've been too afraid to pursue.

Mid-chapter reflection:

What's one small step I can take today to move forward?

What limiting belief do I need to let go of?

Who can I reach out to for support or mentorship?

Remember, growth doesn't happen in comfort zones. It happens when you take that first step—even when you're scared.

Remember, growth doesn't happen in comfort zones. It happens when you take that first step—even when you're scared. But here's the thing people don't talk about enough: growth also occurs when you're surrounded by people who water your potential, not trample it.

Your environment is everything. It can either feed your imposter syndrome or starve it. That's why who you're around matters. Growth is easier when you're around people who speak life into you, challenge you to think bigger, and remind you who you are when you forget. You don't just need hype—you need healthy voices. People who don't just cheer when you win, but pray when you're weary.

One of those people for me is my best friend, Fiona—aka Fee Mak. Fiona is a powerhouse. An established radio presenter who has spoken to millions across the world. A voice-over artist. A dancer. A creative in every sense of the word. But what I love most about her isn't just her resume—it's her heart.

She's been my safe space in seasons where I couldn't see my own greatness. Her words have been seeds that took root in some of my hardest seasons. She has spoken so much life into me—and I've watched her do the same for herself. I remember when she first started out in her presenting career, she battled with doubts. Imposter syndrome tried to convince her that she didn't belong in those rooms, even though her gift said otherwise.

Back then, she didn't always feel comfortable networking. Putting herself out there didn't come easy. But she showed up anyway. She faced the fear. She did the work. And now? Mention Fee Mak in any broadcasting room, and the atmosphere shifts—because her name carries *weight*. She's not just booked and busy; she's blessed and bold.

I'm so proud of her because she made a decision: not to be a product of imposter syndrome but to defeat it. And because of that decision, the world now gets to be blessed by her gift.

So, if you're doubting yourself in a season, check your environment. Get around people who remind you that dreaming big isn't crazy—it's *necessary*. People like Fiona who don't just *do* greatness; they *carry* it. Who doesn't just inspire you with their success but also convict you with their consistency? Because sometimes, all it takes to believe in yourself. . . is being around someone who already does.

Imposter syndrome is a battle, but it's one you can win. It starts with acknowledging your fears, challenging your limiting beliefs, and taking action—even when it feels uncomfortable.

Imposter syndrome doesn't show up out of nowhere. It grows in three specific rooms:

- **Silence**—when you don't feel safe to share your struggle, you start believing you're the only one battling it.

- **Shame**—when something in your past made you feel 'too much' or 'not enough', shame quietly tells you to shrink.

- **Comparison**—when you measure your behind-the-scenes against someone else's highlight reel, you'll always feel like a fraud.

The only way to disarm imposter syndrome is to shine light in those rooms—with honesty, healing, and truth.

You are not an imposter. You are a work in progress; every step you take is a testament to your courage and resilience.

So, go out there and shine. The world needs your voice, your story, and your light.

Journaling Prompt

What is one room you've walked into and felt like you didn't belong—even though you did?

Write down the lie imposter syndrome told you in that moment. Now replace it with the truth.

You didn't get here by accident. You belong, even when you don't feel it.

PART II
The Art of Speaking

4

The HE(ART) of Speaking

———

'Don't speak to ears, speak to hearts'.

— Hayley Mulenda

'A good person produces good things from the treasury of a good heart ... What you say flows from what is in your heart'.

— Luke 6:45 (NLT)

Once you've faced the fear of being a fraud, the next layer isn't your voice—it's your heart. Because imposter syndrome may challenge your place, but unhealed pain can shape your posture. You can only speak with power when your heart is whole. And if you don't deal with what's within, you'll eventually leak it through your words. This chapter isn't just about speaking well—it's about speaking from a place that's been well tended to. Because your voice will only ever go as deep as your healing.

People often ask me what will help their message stand out and what will help them be remembered. There are a lot of tips out there, tips on projecting your voice, working the stage, calling, and responding. All these things work, but speaking is in the heart.

Don't focus on grabbing ears; focus on grabbing the heart. You can have them for an hour if you grab their ear, but if you grab their heart, you have them for life. Maya Angelou once said, 'People will not always remember what you said, but they will always remember how you made them feel'.

How you make people feel is actually determined by your healing. You cannot communicate beyond your own healing. Some people don't speak from their heart—they project from their pain. They're not sharing their story—they're bleeding on the mic. They're not leading—they're bleeding. And that's what I call *bleedership*—when people try to lead, teach, or speak while ignoring the wounds, they've never tended to.

Bleedership happens when people get *promises before the process.* When they receive a platform but haven't done the inner work to sustain it. It's when you're elevated publicly but neglected privately. When your voice gets louder before your heart gets lighter. Right now, the number of unhealed people with platforms is worrying. Not because they're not gifted—but because they're bleeding while building.

We've got influencers influencing from insecurity. Speakers who can stir a crowd but can't sit with their own emotions. Leaders who can pour into others but haven't poured into themselves. If more people prioritised their *healing* as much as they did their *hustle*, the world would be a much safer, softer, and stronger place.

Because here's the truth: if you lead from a wound, you might sound powerful, but you'll move from pain, not purpose. And while your story might be real, your state determines whether it will *heal* or *harm*. There's a difference between speaking from a *scar* and speaking from an *open wound*. A scar says, 'I've been through it, but I've healed'. A wound says, 'I'm still hurting, but I haven't stopped long enough to deal with it'.

In 2018, I lost my cousin, who was tragically stabbed to death. But what caused his death wasn't just the stab wound itself—it was the fact that he didn't even realise he was bleeding. He had been stabbed during a fight, and because of the adrenaline, he kept moving, unaware of the internal damage. By the time he felt weak and realised something was wrong, it was too late. He was rushed to the hospital, but he died upon arrival. The nurses and doctors told us, 'If only he had known earlier . . . if only someone had noticed . . . he would still be alive'. That story haunts me, but it reminds me of what happens spiritually, emotionally, and even communicatively when we don't realise we're bleeding. When you haven't stopped to heal, you can walk into rooms unaware that you're speaking, leading, and relating from a wounded place. The damage goes unnoticed—until you burn out, break down, or hurt others with your unhealed words.

Psychologists have found that unresolved trauma can literally disrupt the way we communicate. It can make us defensive, reactive, guarded, or disconnected. Trauma impacts areas of the brain like the prefrontal cortex—which helps us process and express clearly—and the amygdala, which regulates emotional responses. So, if you haven't healed, your words might sound passionate, but they'll carry more pain than purpose. And people can feel that—even if they can't explain it.

That's why healing has to come before helping. If not, you risk stepping into *bleedership*—showing up to lead but really leaking. I knew I didn't want to be that person. I didn't want to speak from a place that was still bleeding because I understood that unhealed words can unintentionally wound others. But I also knew that silence wasn't the answer either. I had to find the balance to speak *while* healing, but not speak *instead of* healing.

So I once caught myself in the height of bleedership in 2016. I had just turned 18, and my speaking career was scaling massively, but here's the thing: while I was out here speaking life into everyone else's soul, I was quietly neglecting my own. I became so consumed with showing up, encouraging others, and being the 'strong one' that I didn't realise I was abandoning myself in the process. I didn't pause long enough to ask myself, *'But how are you, really?'* The trauma I had experienced over the years—moments I never gave myself space to grieve, understand, or unpack—started to pile up.

I didn't know then that suppression wasn't the same as strength. I bottled things up and kept them moving, thinking purpose would somehow silence my pain. But pain doesn't disappear when you ignore it; it festers. My depression didn't crash in like a storm—it crept in like a fog. Slowly, quietly, and then all at once. By the time 2016 came around, I was 18, and I broke down. Completely. That's why healing has to come before helping.

Trigger Warning: Suicide Attempt

So, in 2016, at the age of 18, I tried to take my life on two separate occasions through an overdose. If I am being honest, at the time when this was happening, I was scared to speak up; I drowned myself in silence and kept telling myself it was not worth sharing how I felt. If I am being honest, I was quite critical of myself, and I was also in denial—'How can someone like me be depressed?'—this is what I would tell myself. The thought of admitting I was depressed and suicidal was quite daunting.

It was in June 2016 that something shifted in me to speak up. I had been off social media for a few months, and I had come across an article online that a young girl from my area, who was 14 years old, had taken her own life. I felt burdened and compassioned because I had just come out of a suicidal place, and I felt there was no one my age really sharing the truth behind suicide attempts and mental health. It was 11 a.m., and I logged into my Snapchat; I don't think I had even brushed my teeth or washed my face.

I started it off by saying, 'Hey guys, I know I have been away for a while, and I thought it was important that I told you guys where I have been and what I have been facing. I have actually been in a place of depression; I didn't really know how to come forward and say it. These past few months have been hard, but I am getting there'. At the time, I had thousands on my Snapchat, and within the next hour, I would get over 200 Snapchat responses to my stories, and 90% of them would be young people saying, 'OMG, Hayley, thank you for sharing this. I have been in a dark place, too', and that moved me.

It moved me because I kept overthinking my message, thinking I had to be an expert, thinking I had to have all the right words and sound the most polished. But what moved people was not my words; it was my heart. It was my passion and my care.

Coming out of that dark place gave me a new sense of purpose. I realised that my survival wasn't just for me—it was for someone else who might be silently suffering, too. I had spent so long hiding my truth out of fear of judgement, but once I saw how my honesty could make others feel seen, everything shifted. 'People don't care how much you know until they know how much you care'—and those messages I received after sharing my journey were a living example of that. They reminded me that my story mattered, even if I didn't come from the most articulate background. I never imagined speaking about mental health in front of CEOs, professionals, or packed auditoriums. But the moment I stopped focusing on how polished it sounded and started focusing on how honest it felt, that's when I was set free.

But here's what I've come to learn: while honesty is the foundation, *articulation* is the vehicle. Once you've let it all out—raw, unfiltered, and from the heart—the next step is learning how to shape it. Because the truth is, how you say something can be just as powerful as what you're saying. Whether it's preparing for a keynote, navigating a job interview, or having a hard conversation with someone you care about, structure helps you steward your story with clarity and intention. It doesn't mean losing the rawness but refining it, so the message lands. You don't need to change who you are to be understood; you just need to learn how to communicate from a place that's both *real and ready*. And that's what I want to help you do next.

Here are some things I want you to think about when imagining what you want to share/say:

- Is what you're trying to say clear?

- Do you want to be formal or informal?

- What feelings do you want people to feel?

- What do you want people to take away?

- Does this sound like you?

Let's break down the questions so you understand the HEART of public speaking.

Clarity is always key, not necessarily for others, but actually for you. If everything is a squiggly line and you can't get your heart out clearly, you will be frustrated and you won't be able to communicate freely.

Is What You're Trying to Say Clear?

Clarity is always key, not necessarily for others, but actually for you. If everything is a squiggly line and you can't get your heart out clearly, you will be frustrated and unable to communicate freely. Clarity isn't about using big words or sounding 'deep'—it's about being understood. The best communicators don't leave room for confusion. They get straight to the point without the verbal gymnastics.

Think about it. How many times have you been in a meeting, someone starts speaking, and five minutes in, you have no clue what they're talking about? You're just there, nodding like, *Yeah . . . profound!* But deep down, you're praying someone else asks for clarification. Don't be that person. Before you speak, ask yourself: *Can this be said more simply? Am I adding unnecessary fluff?* If the answer is yes, chop it down. People will respect your words when you respect their time.

Do You Want to Be Formal or Informal?

There's a time and place for everything. You can't be out here using the same tone in a boardroom that you use at brunch with your girls unless you're trying to get escorted out. The way you communicate should reflect the setting you're in.

If you're in a professional space, be polished but not robotic. Some people think formal means stiff—no! You can be warm, engaging, and still sound professional. On the flip side, if you're in a casual setting, don't be so formal that people feel like they're in a TED Talk when all they asked was 'How was your weekend?'

The key is adaptability. Read the room. If you're speaking at a wedding, you better not sound like you're giving a quarterly finance report, or if you're pitching for investment, don't sound like you're catching up over tea. Speak in a way that makes people feel comfortable, but also in a way that commands respect.

What Feelings Do You Want People to Feel?

Speaking isn't just about what you say; it's about how people feel when you say it. Do you want them to feel inspired? Challenged? Motivated? Comforted? Your words should carry the weight of your intention.

Think of your tone, pace, and delivery like seasoning. The same words can have different effects depending on how they're said. You can say, 'I appreciate you' in a way that makes someone feel valued or in a way that makes them question if you're being sarcastic. Your tone is what makes the difference between a speech that moves people and one that makes them check their phones.

When I first started speaking, I used to think content was everything. But I learned quickly that people don't always remember what you say; they remember how you made them feel. If you speak with passion, people catch it. If you speak with hesitation, people feel it. Make sure your words aren't just heard but *felt*.

What Do You Want People to Take Away?

If people leave your talk, conversation, or even voice note thinking, *That was nice . . . but what was the point?*—you missed it. Every time you speak, ask yourself, *What's the one thing I want people to remember?* If you can't answer that, neither can they.

People are busy. Attention spans are shorter than ever. You have to be intentional about what you're depositing into people's minds. A good communicator knows how to package their message in a way that sticks. It's not about saying the most but capturing the greatest emotions with the fewest words.

I learned this the hard way when I used to over-explain everything (recovering over-explainer here). I'd be so excited to share a story that I'd give unnecessary background, 14 side plots, and a prologue when all they needed was the main lesson. Now, before I speak, I ask: *Is this relevant? Will this help them?* Learn to put yourself in others' shoes as you develop your message.

Does This Sound Like You?

Here's the realest question of them all: Are you actually speaking in *your* voice, or are you performing for approval? Because people can smell inauthenticity from a mile away.

When I first started speaking, I thought I had to sound like those polished, corporate speakers with perfect articulation and zero personality. The moment I dropped the act and spoke in my own rhythm, with my own humour and my own experiences, that's when I started getting booked *and* making an impact.

Your voice is your power. Don't water it down, trying to sound like someone else. If you're naturally funny, use humour. If you're a storyteller, tell stories. If you're more direct, own that. The goal isn't to sound like the 'ideal speaker' but like *you*. When you do, people don't just hear you; they *trust* you.

At the end of the day, great speaking isn't about using the fanciest words, the loudest voice, or the longest speech. It's about clarity, connection, and confidence. When you master that, you don't just speak—you impact.

But impact alone isn't the goal. Because impact without *intention* can still miss the heart.

True communication doesn't just leave an impression—it leaves people different.

If there's one thing this chapter should shout, it's this: *Real communication doesn't just inform—it transforms.* It doesn't stop at transferring knowledge—it moves hearts. It makes people feel seen. Known. Less alone. You can say all the right things, but if your heart's not in it, you haven't spoken—you've just *performed.*

John Maxwell said, 'People may hear your words, but they feel your attitude'. And I've seen it time and time again—people may forget what you said, but they'll never forget how you made them feel. Legacy isn't built on clever lines. It's built on *connection.*

But here's the realest truth: your words will only ever go as deep as your healing.

Because unhealed people don't speak—they spill. They project. They leak. That's why you must prioritise healing before the mic, the message, and the moment. Heal first—so that what you pour out isn't pain but *purpose.*

So, if you've been overthinking how to speak well, stop chasing perfection and start choosing *presence.*

Be present with your story. Present with your scars. Present with your *process*. Because when your heart shows up whole, your message *hits differently*.

Your power isn't in polish—it's in *honesty*. It's healing. It's in the courage to be real. So don't just speak to be heard—speak to be *felt*. That's when walls come down. That's when people lean in. That's when something shifts.

That's the HE(ART) of speaking. And it will always speak louder than words ever could.

Journaling Prompt

Think about the last time you spoke from a place of pain instead of purpose.

What was left unhealed in you that may have leaked through your words?

Now ask yourself: what would it look like to speak from a scar instead of a wound?

Write a short message, prayer, or affirmation to yourself—not as the performer, but as the person—from a heart that's healing and ready to be heard.

5

The Power of Storytelling

'The most powerful person in the world is the storyteller'.

— Steve Jobs

'Tell it to your children, and let your children tell it to their children and their children to the next generation'.

— Joel 1:3 (NIV)

Once your heart is whole, your story becomes a tool for healing—not just for you, but for others. Because when you speak from a place that's been processed, not just experienced, your words don't just land—they linger. That's where storytelling begins. Not with perfect phrasing or dramatic moments, but with honesty. Vulnerability is what turns a story into a mirror, letting others see themselves in what you've survived. If speaking is about impact, storytelling is about intimacy. It's how you turn lessons into light. And your story?

It's not just something you went through—it's something someone else might need to get through.

The most powerful thing you have is your story. Many people shy away from their stories simply because they strive for perfection. One of the things I always say, and I mentioned in the book, is that we shouldn't strive to be role models; we should strive to be real models. If there's anything you remember from childhood, it's stories. You always remember the teacher who told the best stories, or the tales shared with you as a child. Storytelling feeds the inner child. If you want to reach people's hearts, speaking to the inner child will resonate with them for life.

The memories you create in childhood are profound. You will never forget your first favourite teacher, the moment you discovered your favourite colour, or your favourite childhood game. Your joy as a child is what makes you human. Many people grow up forgetting and forsaking their inner child. It is essential to cater to that inner child because it often lives longer than adulthood. Many individuals are unhappy because their inner child is dying, and they have more responsibilities than hobbies. Storytelling brings out the inner child in everyone.

The art of storytelling is about speaking to the heart and the inner child. It involves not just speaking to that place but also speaking from that place—drawing from the stories that ignited you and charged you with inspiration. When you tell a child a story that inspires them, whether it's about Santa Claus or the Tooth Fairy, it is that innocence that gives them hope. Hope is the most powerful thing, and the power of storytelling lies in allowing someone to have hope.

Giving someone hope is the most powerful thing you can do. A story is meant to provide hope, to illuminate a light at the end of the tunnel, and to offer more than one can think or imagine. Personally, I love stories. I am a fable girl. I think about the stories that have taught me the greatest lessons. I shared in the previous chapter how, in 2016, I attempted to take my life; I wanted to share the moment that shifted for me while I was in the deepest state of depression. If I told you a story that helped me overcome depression, would you believe me? Well, it's true: my brother told me a story that changed my life.

On one of my lowest days, the day of my final attempt at overdosing, my brother found me and said, 'Hayley, before you do anything, I know you're in a dark place, but I need you to listen to this story'. He told me about Muhammad Ali, who, when he gets into the ring, is cheered on by everyone. But there comes a time when he gets knocked down, and despite the cheers, it is only Muhammad who has the power to get up and fight. My brother said, 'We can all cheer you on, but it's up to you to get up and fight. I believe you can overcome this'.

It was this story that gave me hope that I could fight and overcome depression. Did I overcome that suicidal place instantly? No, it took time, but hope was the seed.

Since 2016, I have never attempted suicide again. This story is the reason why I have been able to scale my career globally, working with some of the greatest organisations, sharing this very story on some of the biggest stages, and giving people hope. I have had people, including CEOs, cry to me, saying it is the most profound story they have ever heard.

One of the key aspects of storytelling is that it gives people hope and is raw and honest. It meets people where they are before showing them where you want to take them. It is essential to speak from hope and from a place you have lived. People can sense when a story is not genuine.

The art of storytelling also involves helping individuals understand the lessons and takeaways. The takeaway from the Muhammad Ali story is that you have the power to get up and fight. It is your choice. Life can be a struggle, and sometimes it is not a straightforward bounce-back. It may require a process of encouragement and self-talk.

I remember a quote that says, 'If things get better in the end, and if they're not better, then it's not the end'. This story changed my life, and I hope it serves as evidence that you can overcome dark places.

Being real about my experiences, including how depressed I was, is crucial. I lost weight, struggled to eat, and had panic attacks. Many people can resonate with at least one of those experiences, even if they have not faced full-blown depression. They may recall a time of grief or disappointment.

Stories that resonate capture human emotion and the inner child. Honesty and hope allow people to feel at home. Stories provide safe spaces for vulnerability. The power and art of storytelling feed the inner child with hope, allowing people to feel seen and learn in ways they may not otherwise.

I advocate for those who speak with stories and encourage better communication through storytelling. One of my favourite storytellers is actually one of my mentees, Charlene, also known as *Charlene The Poet*. I liken her to a modern-day Lauryn Hill, but Lauryn Hill in her early beginnings: raw, fresh, unfiltered, and full of depth. Charlene is one of the most gifted poets and storytellers I've ever come across. She tells stories of life, womanhood, struggle, faith, and resilience in a way I've never heard before. She has this uncanny ability to mix depth with delight—to bring weighty truths wrapped in humour, rhythm, and flow.

But the reason she's my favourite isn't just because of her talent (and trust me, she is *very* talented). It's because she's having fun. She enjoys what she does. She smiles when she shares. She plays with her words. She dances with the rhythm of her voice. And before I break down how to actually master the art of storytelling, I want to leave you with this: **Storytelling is fun. So have fun.** Don't overthink it. Don't box yourself in. The moment you stop performing and start enjoying, your audience will feel it—and that's when the real connection begins.

So let's dig into the practical parts of storytelling, so when it comes to storytelling, I follow a framework so lessons are always taken away from what is being shared.

Here is the triple T framework.

T—Test

T—Testimony

T—Takeaway

The best stories are layered, and it's so important to include those layers within your storytelling. Starting with the test or trial you've faced allows others to connect with your pain—it reminds people they're not alone. Trials have a way of pulling us together. Pain creates bridges. When we find a common pain point, we find common ground. And that shared ground? That's where transformation and impact begin.

But here's what I've learned: before you share your testimony and speak from the scars, you have to ensure the wounds have been adequately cleaned. A lot of people are projecting, not sharing. And there's a big difference. As I said in the previous chapter, if you don't process what's happened to you, you end up bleeding on people who didn't cut you.

Psychological research shows us this clearly. According to a study published in the *Journal of Traumatic Stress*, unprocessed trauma can lead to emotional dysregulation, which in turn disrupts how we communicate—often causing people to respond to present conversations through the lens of past pain (Ford & Courtois, 2013). Another study in *Psychological Trauma: Theory, Research, Practice, and Policy* found that trauma survivors who haven't engaged in proper processing tend to project their internal distress outwardly, often through reactive or avoidant communication styles (Briere & Scott, 2015).

That's why storytelling isn't just about telling your story—it's about stewarding it. When you process privately, you can present powerfully. But when you skip the healing process, your platform can unintentionally become a place of projection. And that's not ministry—that's a misfire. Healing doesn't mean the pain didn't happen. It means the pain no longer controls the narrative.

The next stage in this framework is *testifying*. You've shared the test—now it's time to testify. While pain connects us, it is triumph that gives people hope. You don't want to just leave people in the valley—you want to show them there's a mountaintop too. When you testify, you take people on a journey. You show them what healing looks like. You help them see what growth sounds like. You remind them that a breakthrough is possible.

And there's actual science to back this. Studies have shown that when people share stories of overcoming adversity, it helps the listener feel more hopeful and increases emotional resilience in the one telling the story. A study published in the *Journal of Positive Psychology* found that sharing positive personal experiences leads to increased well-being and builds stronger relational bonds (Lambert et al., 2013). When you testify, you're not just inspiring—you're transferring hope.

Testifying also builds *relatability*. It bridges the gap between 'them' and 'me'. When someone hears your story and realises you've come through what they're currently facing, something clicks. Their guard comes down. Their heart opens up. Because now it's not just theory—it's lived experience. And *that* is what makes your message land. The testimony is the glue of storytelling. It's the binder that connects your past to someone else's future. When you share that you've overcome, you're giving people a roadmap out of their own struggle—and hope is what you want people to feel.

Psychologist Dan McAdams, in his book *The Redemptive Self*, explains how people who frame their lives around redemption are more likely to experience purpose, life satisfaction, and greater emotional health. Your story of triumph isn't just your story—it becomes a survival guide for someone else.

So when you share, don't just speak from your pain—speak from your *process*. Speak from your *progress*. Show the fruit that grew from what once felt like famine. That's where the power is. That's how healing flows.

The final part of storytelling is all about the takeaway. What are you leaving in the hearts of your listeners when the mic is off, the post is scrolled past, or the room has gone quiet? You've brought them into the pain, you've walked them through the process, you've shown them the power of your testimony—but now, what's the seed you're planting in their soul?

Here's what I've learned: if people leave inspired but not instructed, you've missed an opportunity for real impact. You don't just want them to *feel* something—you want them to *grasp* something. Something they can hold on to. Something they can carry into their Monday morning. Because emotion fades, but truth sticks.

One of the biggest mistakes we can make as storytellers is assuming that people will naturally 'get' the point. But not everyone will read between the lines—you've got to highlight it. Make it clear. Make it simple. Wrap your story in a sentence they'll never forget.

There's research that backs this, too. Psychologist Jerome Bruner found that people are *22 times* more likely to remember a fact when it's wrapped in a story (*Actual Minds, Possible Worlds*, 1986). But here's the key: what sticks isn't the story—it's the *meaning* behind the story. The *takeaway* is what turns a moment into a movement.

In the book *Made to Stick*, Chip and Dan Heath talk about how memorable messages have one thing in common: simplicity with substance. They write, 'If you say three things, you say nothing. Strip your message down to its core and make it stick'. And that's what your takeaway is—your core. Your essence. The heartbeat of why you shared in the first place.

One of my secret ingredients to storytelling? *One-liners*. I've trained myself to summarise the heart of what I want to say in a single line—something punchy, poetic, and powerful. It's the kind of sentence that lives rent-free in someone's mind long after you've left the room. While people may forget paragraphs, they rarely forget a line that hits home.

I'll never forget what one of my mentors said to me after I came off stage years ago:

'That was powerful . . . but what do you want them to remember tomorrow?'

Whew. That humbled me. Because I realised it's not just about what you say; it's about what you *deposit*. Are you leaving behind a quote, a question, a shift in mindset, or a challenge that lingers?

That's the mark of a message that moves people. That's how you make it stick.

So here are some questions to ask yourself:

What's the one thing I want them to hold on to?

What do I want to ignite in them?

What do I want them to *do* with what I've shared?

Because your story is the bridge, but the takeaway is the torch. That's what lights the way forward.

One of the most powerful things you can do to implement this framework in your day-to-day life and become a stronger storyteller is to actually journal. Life can happen so fast that we forget the pivotal parts of our stories.

Take a moment to journal, reflect, and ask yourself questions about your day. What was your highlight? What was your biggest lesson? What broke your heart? What encouraged you? A daily or weekly check-in allows you to record your stories and recognise that every day holds a story. Your life is a collection of stories, a library of experiences. If you learn to zoom out and select the most engaging stories to share, whether in a speaking engagement or a conversation, you can communicate in a way that shows vulnerability and transparency while providing hope, direction, and clarity.

The most specific stories from my childhood revolve around hearing many stories about my dad. My dad passed away when I was three years old. One of the things I always heard from an older cousin is that there is a song called 'Coupé Bibamba' by Awilo Longomba. She would always say my dad would sing it to me, and I am so grateful that I have that memory. Now, whenever I listen to the song, I can't help but think of my dad.

Growing up, I often found myself questioning who I was. My mum is of Ugandan descent, and my dad is Congolese. I did not grow up with my Congolese side, which left me feeling like there was always a part of me that did not honestly know myself. I questioned many vital aspects of my life and identity. Hearing stories about how to present my father has affirmed the narrative that I was loved. When your dad dies young, you often question whether they loved you and how they were with you.

Hearing stories of how present my father was, how much he sang to me, and how much he loved being around me brought me a great deal of peace and comfort as I grew up. Even though my dad was not physically there, those stories provided me with comfort in areas where my dad could not. The stories of my father have shaped my childhood significantly and nourished my inner child. My inner child lacked a father's voice, comfort, and love, but those stories allowed me to feel comfort and peace in ways that, unfortunately, my dad could not fulfil physically. However, those stories were able to provide that fulfilment spiritually and emotionally.

As I've gotten older, I've come to realise that I got the storytelling gift from my mum. The majority of the stories I heard about my dad came from her. My mum has spent hours with me—sometimes late at night, sometimes in passing—telling me stories about her childhood, my childhood, Uganda, her career, and life. Her stories always made me feel full inside. They gave me insight, laughter, and grounding. And somewhere along the way, my love for hearing my mum's stories evolved into a deep passion for *telling* stories—because I wanted to give people that same warm, full feeling inside.

Her stories healed me, and now I tell stories so I can help heal others, too.

Maya Angelou said, 'People won't always remember what you said, but people always remember how you made them feel'. I don't think that hope is found in words; hope is found in the feeling. Hope cannot be a place you're taking them to; it has to be a place you're speaking from. Many people try to bring others to somewhere they have never been. The reason I can let people feel hope through my story of overcoming suicide and depression is that I speak from a place of hope. I speak from a place where I have seen hope and encountered hope. I genuinely believe that hope is both a place and a destination. Hope is the ability to see the light at the end of the tunnel. Because I have seen that light, witnessed tests turn into testimonies, and seen my life and my story turn around, I can speak from that place to say, 'Hey, guys. I was once there, and now I'm not there. You can be there too'.

It is essential to understand that you must speak from that place. This is crucial for your audience and for anyone you are communicating with, as it allows you to let someone know that it is possible. Humans are naturally sceptical and doubtful, and we tend to gravitate towards the negative rather than the positive. It is easier to go downhill than climb uphill; thus, it is easier to be negative than positive. Therefore, pushing hope in your storytelling is essential because it is much easier to propagate doubt. There is already so much doubt in the world, from the news to simply picking up your phone; the news is often filled with negativity.

It is crucial to change the narrative and let people know that if you climb uphill, the most beautiful thing awaits you at the top of the hill. Hope is what gives vision even when there is no sight. One of the most powerful stories I have ever heard is about a man who was a patient in a hospital positioned by the wall. He had a friend in the hospital ward next to him, and he would always say to his friend, 'Oh my gosh, the sun is so beautiful. I wish you were where I am right now, and I wish you could see the sun, the birds, the trees, and the grass'. The way he described it made his friend pray, 'Oh my gosh, one day I hope I can be by the wall so I can see this view'. Unfortunately, his friend passed away, but he was later able to be moved to the wall. When he looked out, he discovered there was no window. Confused, he asked the nurse why there was no window when his friend had spoken to him every day about the beautiful view. The nurse replied, 'Oh, that man was blind'.

The greatest lesson I learned from that was that you have to walk by faith, not sight. I share this story to illustrate that hope isn't always about looking at a circumstance that is physically there. Sometimes, hope is a place you create in your mind, soul, and spirit. If you can speak from that place, you will liberate so many people.

I would say that my personal experiences of storytelling have allowed me to enter rooms for which I initially felt unqualified. I am a young Black girl from inner-city London, coming from a single-parent household and of African descent. Although I was born in London, I am first-generation; my mum migrated to London in the 1990s. I found that my story was powerful enough to be a key to rooms I didn't think I was qualified for. My story proved to me that imposter syndrome is a lie and does not exist. It showed me that I could access places I never comprehended or believed I could reach.

One of the things I always think about is when I was 15 years old and wanted to speak alongside Eric Thomas. I aspired to share the stage with him, as he was the number one motivational speaker in the world during my upbringing and one of the highest-paid Black speakers of our time. I always said I wanted Eric Thomas to be my mentor and to know me. I watched his videos religiously, even though I had no idea how I would meet him. I was in inner-city London, and he was in America, from Detroit. His videos had millions of views, some even hundreds of millions, and I was deeply inspired by his content and voice.

I remember telling myself I would meet him, although I didn't know how. The funny thing is that he is the foreword of this book. I met Eric Thomas once in 2018 and had the opportunity to meet him again in 2024. I shared my story with him, saying, 'Hey, I'm a young girl from London who has been following you, and you inspired me to pursue speaking'. I don't think he fully absorbed what I said the first time because he was so busy. However, during our second meeting in 2024, I was able to tell him my story again, not just to him but also to people around him who could advocate for me. They encouraged him to listen to my story.

I was raw and honest, and being myself while speaking from a place of authenticity, honesty, and transparency allowed us to develop an excellent mentor–mentee relationship. This connection led to him writing the foreword for my book. I would definitely say that storytelling has been my power and my key to entering rooms I once thought were impossible for me to walk into.

A common misconception about storytelling is that it is useless and that being vulnerable is a weakness. Many people believe there is no point in being honest or vulnerable because they fear judgement. I would rather be judged for who I am than for someone I am not. The best thing you can do is be yourself and love yourself enough to embrace your true identity. It is more freeing to be authentic.

Dr Brené Brown captures this essence of storytelling so beautifully in her book, *Daring Greatly*; she reminds us that vulnerability isn't weakness; it's 'uncertainty, risk, and emotional exposure'. And what is storytelling, if not precisely that? It's standing in front of people, whether on a stage or in a quiet conversation, and choosing to share the parts of your journey that weren't polished, filtered, or perfect. It's letting people into your truth without knowing how they'll respond—and doing it anyway.

What makes Dr Brené's work so powerful is that it's not just inspiring; it's backed by research. Her findings show that vulnerability is the birthplace of connection, creativity, and courage. She found that the most wholehearted and resilient people are the ones who dare to be seen—flaws, fears, and all. They don't hide behind perfection; they lean into authenticity. And that's what makes a story stick. People don't connect to the version of you that has it all together—they connect to the version that's real. Because when you share your truth, you give others permission to face theirs, too. That's the power of vulnerability in storytelling.

Make sure the story you are telling is genuinely yours and is real. The misconception that you need to portray a life of more incredible wealth, a perfect relationship, or a fulfilling job can be damaging. If it is not your truth, do not post it. Only share what is true to you and what you believe others need to hear and will resonate with.

Your story is powerful. Never let anything or anyone silence it. Remember, you are a library of stories, and they are worth sharing.

Journaling Prompt

Take a moment to reflect on the stories that have shaped you; both the ones you've lived and the ones you've heard.

- What's one story from your life that you've been afraid to share, but deep down you know someone else could be set free by it?

- Where in your life have you seen pain turn into purpose?

- What's a lesson you've learned through experience that could be someone else's survival guide?

- Who were the storytellers in your life growing up? How did their stories make you feel—and what did they awaken in you?

- If someone gave you the mic today, what story would you tell—and what would you want people to take away?

Write freely. Be honest. Be raw. This isn't about performance; it's about permission. Your story doesn't have to be perfect to be powerful. It just has to be true.

6

Speaking to the Right People: Your Customer vs. Your Audience

———

'I'm not saying I'm going to change the world, but I guarantee that I will spark the brain that will change the world'.

— Tupac Shakur

'The purposes of a person's heart are deep waters, but one who has insight draws them out'.

— Proverbs 20:5 (NIV)

Not every voice is meant for every room, and that's okay. One of a speaker's most liberating revelations is this: you are not called to everyone but to someone. The sooner you embrace that truth, the clearer your message will become and the more potent your impact will be. Before crafting messages or curating slides, take a step back and ask yourself: *Who am I really speaking to?* Without this clarity, even the most passionate message can fall on deaf ears.

When it comes to speaking, it is essential to create profiles of the people you are called to address. By profiles, I mean that many people believe they can speak to everyone, but I believe in the power of niching down and understanding your audience. You must create a profile of your audience because you cannot engage with people you do not know or care about. People do not care how much you know until they know how much you care.

You need to discern who you are called to speak to and who burdens your heart. Everyone has a different group of people they care about. For example, I am passionate about young people, especially those from impoverished areas. Growing up in inner-city London, I lived in one of the poorest boroughs, and came from a single-parent household. I grew up in what we call 'the hood'. I love helping young people from similar backgrounds who may not have been shown the right path or who did not know that success was possible for them. I want to help them understand that it is possible to enter spaces where they may not feel qualified or where they may not look like everyone else.

Identifying the people you are called to serve is rooted in your burden. The first step is to determine who you are burdened for. Who are the individuals that tug at your heart in a way you cannot comprehend? That is the most important question.

The second step is to think more deeply about them in terms of their interests, who they listen to, and what type of music they enjoy. This is where profiling begins. You start to identify the people you feel called to impact and speak to. It is crucial to describe that profile in detail. Consider what they like and what type of content they enjoy, and even give your profile a name. For example, you might name someone 'Jerry'.

Ask yourself questions about Jerry: How old is he? What does he like to do? What does he enjoy eating? What type of friends does he have? What does he aspire to be? Is he in university? What religion does he subscribe to? Is he an extrovert or an introvert? What are his biggest struggles and pain points? Does he have his mom in his life? Does he come from a single-parent household?

Answering these questions allows you to develop a detailed profile. When you think about your message and the things you are called to say, you can consider whether your message will impact Jerry. Many people assume that just because their message is good, it will engage the audience. However, having a message that could impact the masses does not guarantee that it will resonate with the specific people you are called to reach.

It is crucial to understand that profiling and asking yourself these questions about your audience will help you better understand who you are called to serve. Ultimately, it is all about service. You must ensure that you are hitting the nail on the head and not just shadowboxing. Shadowboxing refers to boxing the air without a target. You must know exactly who you are addressing to make a real impact and reach people's hearts.

The best way to direct your messages is to focus on individuals. When speaking to a particular audience, look for the 'Jerry' in the room. Once you impact one Jerry, other Jerrys will emerge, and you may also discover a Tom or a Darren. This process will provide you with more insight into your audience and the people you are called to impact.

One of the reasons I became passionate about helping young people from my area is that your level of exposure determines your level of success. My exposure was limited because my school and the environment I grew up in lacked the resources to introduce me to better opportunities. Unfortunately, the things I was exposed to growing up included gang affiliation. I witnessed people being raped, stabbed, and shot in my neighbourhood. I had neighbours who were drug dealers, and I grew up with individuals who ended up in jail for violent crimes or who we mourned at funerals due to gang-related violence.

The type of exposure I had was primarily one of crime and poverty, reinforcing the notion that this is the area you grow up in and the area you die in. I became passionate about showing young people that just because they lived there does not mean they have to stay there or that they are products of their environment. I do not believe you are a product of your environment; rather, you are a product of your vision. I wanted to change the vision that young people were seeing. When I started to dream bigger, travel more, and expose myself to different environments, teachings, and literature, my circumstances changed. I wanted to be the voice I needed when I was younger, which fuelled my passion for helping young people from impoverished areas. I recognised that this was not only what I needed but also saw others around me who had taken certain paths. I wondered if they had received earlier intervention, perhaps they would not have made choices detrimental to their well-being.

I felt it was important to identify specifically what type of young person I wanted to cater to because I do not believe every young person from impoverished areas is cut from the same cloth. Additionally, I wanted to avoid the saviour complex of trying to save everyone, as that would only lead to my own burnout and deficit. Defining the niche of people you are called to serve, speak to, and impact is crucial. By doing so, you allow yourself the grace to be more direct and protective of your energy, preventing burnout and ensuring you do not end up in a deficit.

Profiling is the ability to create profiles, just like how organisations have information about their clients. They understand their clients' trends and habits. This concept also applies to you, not just in a transactional commercial context but in a transactional impact context. Directing your impact to the right person is essential to ensure they benefit from your words, messages, and the things you are called to convey.

Many people, when they start sharing their stories, realise they have been helping the wrong individuals. Those with big hearts often get hurt because they care for people who take their energy and love without reciprocating. Profiling begins with understanding what type of person you are and what you offer. This is similar to the concept of love languages, as discussed by Gary Chapman. Understanding your love language helps you communicate effectively and meet someone else's love language.

The different love languages include gifts, physical touch, words of affirmation, and quality time. Understanding your love language and speaking style will make it easier for you to profile those you are called to impact. First, consider the type of person you are. Are you focused on words of affirmation? If you struggle with insecurity, you may become a speaker seeking affirmation from your audience rather than aiming to impact them. It is crucial to address any insecurities related to words of affirmation.

If you prioritise quality time, you may develop inappropriate boundaries with those you are meant to mentor. You might seek validation and proximity with individuals you should love or coach from a distance. Knowing who you are is vital before describing who you are called to impact. Once you understand your love languages and how you show love, impact, and encouragement, it is also important to recognise your speaking style.

Not all speakers speak the same—and not all impact is made in the same way.

Depending on your purpose, your audience, and the message you're carrying, your speaking style might fall into one of these four categories: **motivational, inspirational, informational,** or **transformational**.

Some people may blend between styles, but understanding these distinctions can help you own your voice and sharpen your message.

Motivational Speaking

Motivational speakers aim to ignite and energise their audience, often in high-paced environments like sales, finance, or sports, where intense pressure requires consistent encouragement. They push people to take immediate action, overcome laziness, or break free from limiting beliefs.

Example: Eric Thomas (ET the Hip-Hop Preacher)

I've mentioned ET a few times in this book already—and rightly so. You simply cannot talk about motivational speaking without mentioning him. Eric Thomas changed the entire paradigm of what it means to be a motivational speaker. His high energy, raw passion, and authentic delivery have made him a staple in locker rooms, boardrooms, and school assemblies across the world. He doesn't just hype you up—he wakes something up *within* you. His iconic line, 'When you want to succeed as bad as you want to breathe', isn't just a quote—it's a cultural reference point for drive and determination. ET made motivation not just powerful but also personal.

Inspirational Speaking

Inspirational speaking is deeper and characterised by storytelling, transparency, and emotional connection. It often involves communicating traumatic or profound themes, requiring vulnerability to foster connection and impart lessons. It's not just about stirring emotions—it's about stirring transformation through truth.

Example: Inky Johnson

Inky Johnson is a masterful inspirational speaker whose story grips you from the moment he starts speaking. A former college football star with dreams of going pro, Inky's life changed overnight when a career-ending injury left his right arm permanently paralysed. But instead of allowing that moment to break him, he used it to *build others*. Inky's messages go far beyond sports—he speaks about faith, character, perseverance, and identity. His delivery is raw, heartfelt, and deeply moving. Inky doesn't just tell you to keep going—he *shows* you what it looks like to walk through pain with purpose. His story reminds us that sometimes the biggest breakthroughs come through what looks like a breakdown.

Informational Speaking

Informational speaking focuses on facts rather than emotions. It's research-based, analytical, and rooted in frameworks or data. These speakers aim to educate, not just inspire—offering the audience new knowledge, tools, and insight that can be practically applied.

Example: Dr Caroline Leaf

Dr Caroline Leaf is a cognitive neuroscientist and mental health expert who has dedicated over 30 years to studying the mind-brain connection. Her gift lies in making science simple. She breaks down complex neurological and psychological concepts in a way that's not only digestible but also deeply empowering. Dr Leaf doesn't just talk about what's happening in the brain— she teaches people how to *retrain* it. Whether she's speaking about toxic thought patterns, trauma recovery, or mental resilience, her insights are always grounded in research and practical application. Her work shows that transformation doesn't just require inspiration—it requires information.

Transformational Speaking

Transformational speaking is geared towards those engaged in mindset work, organisational change, or system-level impact. These speakers don't just inspire—they *reconstruct*. They challenge you to unlearn, rethink, and realign. Their words shift cultures, restructure organisations, and reframe how people see themselves and the world around them.

Example: Dr Myles Munroe

Dr Myles Munroe was more than a speaker—he was a reformer. His teachings on purpose, leadership, and kingdom principles didn't just inspire people—they transformed nations, businesses, and ministries. He had a rare ability to speak to CEOs and presidents while still being able to teach a child in Sunday school. Myles didn't just speak for applause—he spoke for alignment. His words left people walking away not just encouraged but *equipped*. He was a master at pulling people out of survival mode and into legacy thinking. He didn't just speak to the mind—he activated purpose in the soul.

Each type of speaker holds power in their own way. Some stir action, some stir healing. Some bring clarity, and others bring complete transformation. Your voice may not fit neatly into one box—and that's okay. What matters is that you understand the **intention** behind your voice and the **impact** it's called to make. Whether you're here to motivate, inspire, inform, or transform— own your lane. Because the moment you do, your message doesn't just land—it *leads*.

Identifying your love languages and speaking style will enhance your understanding of yourself and those you are called to impact. This self-awareness helps you recognise who would benefit from your services, love language, and speaking style. Profiling begins with defining who you are, what you carry, your gifts, strengths, love languages, and personality. This understanding allows you to identify who you are burdened by and who would benefit from the type of person you are.

A lot of people reach a point where they wonder if having a particular niche means they cannot speak to or impact those who don't look like them or who they are not necessarily burdened by. I would argue that, although all humans are different, we are very similar in nature. Any healthy human being would feel upset upon hearing that a young person has been hurt, or they would be moved by catastrophes or wars. There is compassion for those who are vulnerable and those who have been innocently hurt by catastrophic events.

It is essential to find common ground that can be leveraged to connect people. In my speaking style, the common ground is laughter. I always try to make people laugh because I believe laughter is medicine for the soul. I aim to reference macro trends—those things that are trending on a mass scale—rather than making jokes that only I or a few people in the room might understand.

When addressing audiences that may not sound or look like you, it is crucial to conduct research about them. Understand what they may be interested in and what topics they might want to discuss. It is perfectly acceptable to be a student of your audience. I personally suggest that being a student of audiences is important because it helps break down prejudices and misconceptions or fears you may have about them. Ultimately, this approach allows you to avoid generalising everyone as the same type of listener.

Every audience has a different listening style, and every individual listens differently. Some people listen through kinetic movements, some through visual cues, and others through audio alone. Studying the types of people who may differ from your ideal audience provides greater insight into how you can impact them. This effort ensures that they do not feel that you are being lazy in your delivery or engagement.

In the end, the process of profiling and narrowing your audience isn't about boxing yourself in—it's about freeing your message. When you speak to the right people, with the right heart, your voice carries greater weight. Your words can have the most meaningful influence in that space of focused clarity. So, take the time to reflect, to listen, and to discern. When you know who you are truly called to reach, you won't just speak to their ears—you'll speak to their hearts.

Journaling Prompt

Who are the people I feel most burdened for, and why?

What specific traits, challenges, or dreams do they have?

How does my personal story equip me to serve and speak to them?

PART III
The Science Behind Speaking

7

Personal Branding— Your Greatest Asset in a Noisy World

'A good name is more desirable than great riches; to be esteemed is better than silver or gold'.
— Proverbs 22:1 (NIV)

'If people like you, they will listen to you, but if they trust you, they'll do business with you'.
— Zig Ziglar

Personal brand is the new currency—it is now what deems you credible, and it's now something people are looking for when you're trying to build a digital brand. A brand is not built in a day; it's something you must build daily. There has to be a daily commitment to your personal brand simply because the personal brand isn't in the result; it's in the journey.

People don't just want to know who you are; they want to know the back story; they want the who, what, where, how, why, and when. A strong personal brand reveals that without being too explicit. A question a lot of people ask is, 'Can I still build a personal brand whilst still being private?' The answer is yes. You choose the parameters around your personal brand; the power is in your hands; never be afraid to build a brand because you're worried about who might know your business; you still get to choose the cards you play—don't let the internet fool you.

I didn't even realise I was doing it when I started building my brand! I had no idea that simply showing up, sharing my thoughts, and religiously posting my videos on social media would become my most valuable currency. I didn't realise that people were actually watching me and referring to me for opportunities; I just thought I was sharing; I didn't know that sharing would actually change my life and put me into opportunities that would change my life for good. In 2024, I had a viral video that added around 60,000 followers to my Instagram in the space of one week; it was because I said the term, 'you're too broke to not be visible', and I stand by it. You're too broke not to be visible.

There is so much power in visibility. If you're invisible, then you're not visible—as some may say, closed mouths do not get fed. If you want to get paid, you must be seen. We live in a time where visibility isn't just for celebrities or influencers; it's for everyone. It's for those who want to make a change and actually want to make a difference. It's for those who want impact and for those who want to be a voice.

People no longer buy into products or services; they buy into **people**. They buy into your humanity, transparency, and vulnerability. Dr Brené Brown says, 'Trust is built in very small moments'. This means every post, conversation, and action contributes to your brand's trustworthiness.

As I said earlier, a personal brand is not built in a day; it's built daily. However, many people forget that the most important word in personal branding is 'person'. You have to learn the importance of showing up online and offline.

The belief that personal branding is only about your social media presence, following, and online persona is a huge trap that many people fall into. Building your personal brand offline is just as important. Your offline, personal brand is built by your network, values, credibility, and character.

Have you ever heard about a celebrity who appeared to be kind or nice online, but you've heard stories about them being a diva or a completely different person? This can easily happen to you if you don't have a mirror and a C.O.R.E.—when you're working out, one of the most important parts of the body you must build strength in is the core.

The C.O.R.E. is easy to neglect because you don't see it, but just because you don't see, it doesn't mean it's not important.

What is the C.O.R.E for your personal brand?

Character—Opportunities—Relationships and Evidence

C—Character

Who are you when no one is watching?

There have been different times throughout the book where I have stated that integrity is everything and the most important thing to have. Your integrity, attitude, and how you treat others in everyday situations shape your personal brand more than anything else. Your character will speak for you louder than your accolades. People take tabs on their interactions with you—whether it's a good day or a bad day, they're taking notes on how you handle your different seasons. We all face different seasons in life.

We face the spring seasons—our spring season is when we are just breaking out and on the verge of a breakthrough. People watch how you act when you're nearly there. People will watch how resilient you are if you speak about motivation and resilience. People watch to see whether you will crumble or not.

We face the summer seasons—this is when everything is thriving and things are working well for you—people will watch whether your pride and ego scream loud—your humility will speak for you in the summer.

We face the fall/autumn seasons, which is when things start to close and things start to fall apart. People watch for bitterness and watch whether you will project, and it's the same for the final season—winter when NOTHING is happening for you.

How do you treat people through your seasons? Do you disregard people and let your ego speak for you in your spring and summer seasons? Or, in your winter/fall season, does your bitterness or projection speak for you?

If there's anything to take away: Be kind, even when inconvenient.

O—Opportunities (How You Show Up in Rooms)

Where are you positioning yourself?

Your presence in real-life environments—events, meetings, casual gatherings—either reinforces or reshapes your brand. Show up prepared, engaged, and ready to contribute, not just consume.

When you hear someone speak, do you clap? Do you affirm them in what they've shared? When you're networking, do you only speak about yourself or give them space to share their story and thoughts? When brought into an opportunity, are you only thinking about what you can gain? Or are you thinking of how to be a blessing, serve, and add value?

This is something you need to focus on, and this is something you need to consider.

If there's anything to take away, be intentional in every room you enter. Focus on adding value, and you'll always be memorable.

R—Relationships (Your Network and Reputation)

What do people say about you when you're not in the room? Your network often carries your name further than you can.

Your offline brand is rooted in being someone others can confidently refer to or recommend. Most people want to be confident that if they're putting you forward for an opportunity, you won't embarrass them. Trust is not given; it is earned.

You need to ensure you're showing up how you want people to introduce you. If you want to be introduced as a speaker, you better be speaking. If you want to be introduced as a swimmer, you better know how to swim. Are you doing what you want to be introduced as? Do people see it, and do they feel comfortable sharing it?

If there's anything to take away, your reputation is everything.

E—Evidence (Credibility and Results)

What have you actually done?

Your results, work ethic, and experiences speak for you. Whether testimonials, word of mouth, or a track record of excellence, credibility is built over time and rooted in real-life outcomes.

Some people want an endorsement for wishful thinking—that isn't work. Do the work and let your results speak for you.

Let your work talk louder than your words if there's anything to take away.

Now that we have dealt with offline personal branding, we can deal with online personal branding.

In the digital age, where social media and digital consumption are at an all-time high, it is so important to take your place and define your lane online. Social media is a powerful medium through which you can establish yourself as a voice in our generation. Many overlook social media's power and the impact of posting content. Those who are seen are the ones who get booked. Personal branding isn't just a nice-to-have; it's essential in today's world. If you're not building your personal brand, you're giving up the power to shape your narrative online.

There was a time when your work alone could speak for you, but now it does help to have an online profile that can amplify it. The digital space has created an attention economy—the more visible and credible you are, the more opportunities you attract. According to a study by LinkedIn, 75% of professionals believe that having a strong personal brand is key to career growth. Another report by Edelman Trust Barometer found that people are three times more likely to trust an individual than a brand. People would rather buy from, work with, and invest in you—not just your business.

I remember that, in 2018, I was approached by an organisation to speak at Wembley Arena. They reached out via email after coming across a video of mine. As a result of that video, they were interested in having me speak at one of their events in front of 16,000 people. At that time, the largest audience I had spoken to was about a hundred people. I was just starting my speaking career and was only 19 years old. When I received that email, I was in disbelief. I responded immediately, expressing my interest and asking how they found out about me. They mentioned they used SEO on YouTube, typed 'mental health speaker', and my name appeared.

I looked at that video, which had only 50 views. Many people think success is about the number of views, but it only takes one person to see you for your life to change. I didn't have a hundred thousand views or even 10,000, but one of those 50 views belonged to the organisation's program director hosting the event at Wembley Arena. In 2018, I spoke at Wembley Arena at 19 in front of 16,000 people, the largest audience I've ever addressed. This opportunity arose simply because I was visible; I didn't watch the views; I just focused on adding value.

I have been consistently posting content for the past 12 years. When I first started speaking at 15, I posted my videos on YouTube. Was I perfect? No. Was it the best content? No. However, I learned that when people become engrossed in your content and invested in you, they will explore your journey.

When I think about the power of following someone's journey, I can't include one of my close friends and someone I often work with quite closely, Blessing, aka Annatoria. Annatoria is a multi-award-winning gospel sensation. She won The Voice UK at the age of 17 in 2020, and she has won the hearts of millions. Since then, she has gone on to build a very big social media following— at the time I am writing this book, her social media following is just under two million followers across her Instagram, TikTok, and YouTube. Blessing often posts videos of her singing covers and singing different songs, sometimes her own music and sometimes others— she is probably the most diligent person I know when it comes to content—she never shies away from her personality, and she makes an effort to engage with her followers, fans, and comments. I have seen first-hand how visibility has changed her life; there have been so many musical and personal opportunities presented to her just because she decided to show up online and build an amazing personal brand. There have been moments when we have been on long car journeys, and she has whipped out her DJI OSMO Pocket 3 or her MacBook so she can edit; she prides herself on being consistent in posting, and she's someone who taught me the power of content and visibility.

Can I be honest? There are quite a few individuals who go on TV talent shows and end up being forgotten because they make no effort to build their personal brand afterwards. Blessing didn't let the show carry her brand; she built it for herself—allowing people to know her beyond winning The Voice UK and engaging with her personality and core values. I had the pleasure of helping her plan her first headline show in Accra, Ghana; this was a big deal because she is not of Ghanaian heritage—she is a British Zimbabwean girl . . . But VISIBILITY! Visibility was her key to branching out into the world and tapping into limitless opportunities. Her personal brand is one of the strongest I have seen, and this wasn't someone who had any label backing or financial aid; all she had was the heart to show up and all the opportunities showing out for her.

Blessing has won many awards, one of them being a MOBO award, one of the most prominent UK music awards. She has encountered life-changing opportunities and built up credibility amongst gospel legends because she is visible, and they've seen her content everywhere. Suppose there's something I would say I really do admire about Blessing. In that case, it is that she is going to show up, regardless of what is happening—she will show up because she knows her career depends on it, and she is not afraid to show her personality—her most viral videos that have received millions of views haven't always been her singing; it's sometimes being comical and just having fun and showing her personality.

People no longer connect with profiles; they want to connect with individuals. It is crucial to ensure that your personal brand reflects your humanity. Blessing shows her humanity, and that's why she gets her followers. I have said it before and will say it again—you cannot have a personal brand without the word 'person'. Many people focus on aesthetics and editing while neglecting the human aspect behind the brand.

So let's get practical with building your personal brand—

- First, be content with posting regularly, whether once a week or once a day. Find a rhythm and stick to it.

   Many people become discouraged after their first attempt at posting, thinking they don't get enough views. However, if you remain consistent, those views will accumulate. Consistency helps you build a community, establish a pattern, and create a routine.

- Second, stop caring about what others think. There is a scripture I love that says the fear of man is a snare (Proverbs 29:25). Many people hold themselves back due to the opinions of others. You must walk unapologetically in what you post and understand that not everyone will support or understand what you stand for, and that is okay.

- Third, stop waiting for the opportunities and be okay with building your own. When I first started speaking, I wasn't waiting for someone to give me a platform—I built my own. I created content, I hosted my own events, and I made sure people associated my name with value. That's what a personal brand does—it precedes you, promotes you, and positions you before you even step into the room.

- Fourthly—focus on the audience you feel called to impact and double down on those connections.

- Finally—do not neglect analytics. Evaluate your insights on platforms like Instagram and LinkedIn. Numbers do not lie. Determine what posting times work best and which posts have the highest engagement—my husband Sterling taught me about the importance of analysing.

It would be impossible to talk about insights, and I do not mention my husband, Sterling Record. Sterling actually got me into building my social media profile—I wasn't too bothered by algorithms and posting until we got together. When I first got with my husband, he was an accountant who was obsessed with numbers, and when he started getting into marketing, he applied the same analytical skills from his accounting background, and he applied them to marketing.

Sterling taught me that visibility is in the analytics and visibility is in the numbers—the insights do not lie. Many people want to be visible without actually looking at their insights and analytics—your visibility has to be built on the insight behind what's working and what is not.

Sterling brought an awareness to me—an awareness of a digital world that I tried pushing away but could no longer run away from. I needed to address the truth. Social media is changing the way we do life, and if I don't look into it properly, it will be a waste of time and not something that works in my favour.

Sterling taught me that it's essential to evaluate before you elevate. Many rush to the next level without assessing their current position. Take the time to evaluate what is working and what is not, rather than feeding your ego.

Be cautious not to seek affirmation or validation through visibility. Human opinions are fickle; one day, people may praise you, and the next, they may criticise you. Remember that the same people who shouted 'Hosanna' for Jesus were the same ones who called for his crucifixion.

I said it earlier in the book: do not let criticism get to your heart, and don't let compliments get to your head; protect your ego. It is actually vital to remain humble. Being seen does not make you a god or immune to life's challenges; it amplifies your voice and allows you to stand for something greater than yourself, impacting others as a voice of change.

Now that we've explored the foundation of your offline brand through the C.O.R.E. framework—character, opportunities, relationships, and evidence—it's time to shift gears and tackle your online presence. Offline will keep your name noble, but online will keep your name known. And let me be real with you: in our world, you can't afford to be invisible.

The digital world isn't slowing down, and if you want to remain relevant, respected, and remembered, you must be strategic about how you present yourself online. This isn't about perfection or performance—it's about being intentional.

So, let me introduce you to the same system I've taught to clients, CEOs, and creatives worldwide. It's helped me build a platform that speaks even when silent.

I Call It V.I.S.A.

Because just like a visa gives you access to new territory, this framework helps give your voice access to new rooms, relationships, and revenue.

V—Visibility

Can people find you online?

Visibility is about consistently showing up in the spaces where your audience hangs out—whether that's LinkedIn, Instagram, YouTube, or a personal blog. It's not just about being seen once but being seen regularly in a way that builds recognition.

Sometimes, all it takes is *doubling down on one platform* to build an undeniable presence. Take MrBeast, for example. He became one of the most recognisable content creators in the world by focusing obsessively on YouTube. He mastered one platform, and now his brand transcends platforms and industries.

Or look at Kai Cenat. He didn't try to be everything to everyone. He committed to Twitch, showed up consistently, and built such a powerful presence that it naturally spilt over into other platforms, opportunities, and global recognition.

Tip: Pick 1–2 platforms you can consistently show up on. Don't try to be everywhere. Be where it matters—and be there with purpose.

I—Identity

What do you want to be known for?

Your brand identity includes your message, tone, values, and visuals. It's the essence of who you are and how you consistently communicate that across your content. Authenticity is key—people connect to *real*, not *rehearsed*.

Look at Tony Robbins. His identity is unmistakable. Everything he touches emphasises peak performance, mindset, leadership, and transformation. From his voice to his stage presence, from his books to his social media—he embodies what he teaches.

Tony doesn't confuse his audience with mixed messages; he reinforces his mission. And that clarity is what has built global loyalty and impact.

Tip: Choose 2–3 themes that reflect your expertise and personality (e.g., leadership, faith, communication). Let your content revolve around these. When people think of your name, they should immediately connect it to what you stand for.

S—Storytelling

Are you connecting or just posting?

Great personal brands don't just inform—they connect emotionally. Your story, your lessons, your journey, your voice—that's what makes your brand relatable and memorable. People don't follow brands; they follow *people*. They follow *how* you make them feel.

One person who does this beautifully is Tabitha Brown. She didn't build her platform by trying to be perfect—she built it by being present. Whether she's cooking, praying, laughing, or sharing her struggles, her tone feels like a warm conversation.

Her storytelling is honest, simple, and full of soul. She's built a brand that connects deeply with millions because she dares to be vulnerable and visible simultaneously.

Tip: Share behind-the-scenes moments, wins, challenges, and transformations. Let people see the process, not just the polished outcome. People relate to your journey more than your highlight reel.

A—Authority

Why should people trust you?

Authority turns followers into clients, audiences into communities, and content into credibility. It's built on value, evidence, and results.

Take Simon Sinek. He didn't go viral overnight, but his *'Start with Why'* concept became a movement. He focused on thought leadership—writing, speaking, teaching—and created consistent value that resonated across industries.

His authority wasn't based on volume—it was based on depth. Simon has spoken on global stages, advised world-class companies, and earned trust because he brings clarity, insight, and impact every single time he shows up.

Tip: Share educational content, highlight results and testimonials, collaborate with trusted voices, and let people see not just what you do but what you've *helped others do*. Authority grows through trust, and trust grows through consistency.

So here's what I want to leave you with: V.I.S.A. + C.O.R.E.

That's the balance. One is what makes you visible; the other is what makes you valuable.

Getting caught up in the likes, views, and followers is easy. But here's what I know: *real brands aren't just built in the feed—they're built in the fibre of who you are.*

Visibility might get you in the room.

But the character will keep you there.

The content might start the conversation.

But connection will make people remember your name.

So yes, post with purpose. Share your story. Build your platform.

But more importantly—protect your name. Let your life reflect what your content says.

Your integrity will be remembered when the algorithm changes and the trends fade.

The personal brand is not about being perfect but consistent, credible, and clear.

And the most powerful brand you will ever build is the one that looks like you.

Your personal brand isn't just your platform—it's your pattern. It's how you move, how you love, how you lead, and how you live when no one is watching. It's the echo of your integrity and the evidence of your consistency. In a world that's constantly shouting for attention, your brand should whisper something deeper: *trust me*. Because the most powerful brands aren't built through virality—they're built through *values*. You don't need to copy anyone else. You just need to own who you are and show up for the people you're called to serve. The world doesn't need another perfect profile—it needs a real person with purpose.

If someone were to describe *your* personal brand without mentioning your job title, followers, or platform—what would they say about you?

Journaling Prompt

Reflect on how your **character, consistency, and content** are shaping the way people experience your name. What adjustments do you need to make to ensure that your personal brand reflects the person you truly are?

8

Your Community Is Your Currency

'We were created for community, fashioned for fellowship, and formed for a family'.

— Rick Warren

'Carry each other's burdens, and in this way you will fulfil the law of Christ'.

— Galatians 6:2 (NIV)

In today's digital world, having followers is no longer enough. Anyone can go viral, gain thousands of followers overnight, or even buy an audience. But the real question is: Can you turn that audience into a community? Can you build something that lasts beyond the algorithm?

I've seen this play out in my own journey. Over the years, I've built a community that goes beyond just numbers. Whether through my Equipped Movement, where I bring together people of faith for fellowship and personal growth, or through my Equipped Dubai events that create safe spaces for expats to connect, I've witnessed the power of real, engaged communities.

The Equipped Movement isn't just a ministry—it's a family. It's a Christian fellowship that exists to help believers be equipped for their calling, both spiritually and practically, especially in the marketplace. It's a space where people come to be sharpened, strengthened, and stretched in their faith. And one thing I've learned is this: consistency is what earns trust. Trust isn't given— it's earned. And I've spent nearly a decade earning it.

Before I ever launched Equipped, I had already spent almost a decade consistently showing up—running public speaking workshops, training sessions, and youth-focused events across the United Kingdom and beyond. These were separate from my ministry work and were rooted in helping people—especially young people— develop their communication skills, build confidence, and find their voice. I led corporate training sessions, hosted youth development events, and created safe spaces where people could grow in personal power. I poured into people's lives not to be seen, but to see them win. That consistency didn't just build my credibility—it built my community.

Because of community, I've been able to speak across the Middle East, Europe, Africa, and the United States. I've been invited to rooms I never even applied for. Why? Because communities advocate for you when you're not in the room. People didn't just follow me—they believed in the mission and carried it further than I ever could have on my own.

But what really sets a community apart from an audience?

An audience listens. A community responds. An audience watches. A community shows up. An audience may scroll. A community takes action.

You can have 100,000 followers, but if you can't sell 10 tickets to an event or get 50 people to join a live session, you don't have a real community. Influence is not measured by numbers—it's measured by impact. And when your people feel connected to your mission, they move with you.

That's why someone with 10,000 engaged followers can outsell someone with a million passive ones. Community is not about who follows you—it's about who's willing to build with you.

What draws people together isn't just content. It's conviction. It's vision. If you want people to gather, you have to give them something to rally around.

Look at Stormzy. He didn't just rise because of music. Stormzy, a British rapper, singer, and songwriter, became a household name not just for his sound but for his stance. He's vocal about his Christian faith, unapologetically Black, and deeply invested in social justice. Through his #Merky Foundation, he's funded scholarships for Black students at Cambridge, advocated for underrepresented communities, and used his platform to amplify voices that need to be heard. His community didn't just stream his music—they stood with his message. They saw themselves in his story, and that created a movement.

Or Kai Cenat, one of the most influential content creators of Gen Z. He's not just known for his viral Twitch streams or comedic YouTube videos—he's known for how he makes people feel included. Kai built his digital empire by being consistent, relatable, and interactive. His audience doesn't just watch him—they feel like they're part of something. Whether he's streaming for hours or engaging in chaotic group chats, he invites his community to be part of the journey, not just spectators. He transformed digital engagement into digital belonging. His audience feels like insiders, not just observers. They show up because they feel seen.

And that's the key: clarity of mission attracts your tribe. The more you stand for, the more people can stand with you.

When I launched Equipped, I wasn't just starting another event—I was building a sanctuary. A place for people of faith to be poured into and be reminded they're not alone.

This wasn't about performance—it was about presence. I stayed consistent. I made myself accessible. I didn't just produce content; I created moments. Prayer calls, online fellowships, Bible studies—everything was built to cultivate connection.

And the result? People didn't just engage with me; they engaged with each other. They felt seen. They grew together. And, most importantly, they stayed.

So how do you keep people engaged in a world filled with distractions?

You show up. You listen. You build tradition. Whether through Q&As, voice notes, or reposts—your consistency builds trust.

Ask your community questions. Give them ways to participate. Make them feel like part of the story.

Create spaces where people feel like they belong. Give them shared language, recurring touchpoints, and reasons to keep coming back.

And never underestimate the power of a direct message, a response to a comment, or a public shout-out. Small touches leave lasting impressions.

Now let's talk about ownership. You can't build a lasting community on a rented platform. Algorithms shift. Accounts get disabled. But your email list? Or private community? That's legacy.

Start capturing emails through value. Offer what serves. Make it easy. Make it meaningful. And don't ghost your list. Show up in inboxes with value, not just offers.

To make this easier, use tools that streamline the process and give your people better experiences—whether it's email marketing platforms, community hubs, or monetisation tools that allow you to serve deeper.

When you serve with intention, you don't just build followers—you build family. And when that happens, you no longer need to chase validation. You're rooted in community.

When people feel seen, they stay. When people feel heard, they show up. And when people feel valued, they become advocates.

So if you're building a community—start with connection, lead with service, and nurture with care. Because the ones who walk with you now are the ones who'll carry your name further than you ever could on your own.

1. **Start with Your Why**

    Before the tools and tech, get clear on your *why*. What's the purpose of your community? Is it to teach? Connect? Empower? Encourage? When people understand the *why*, they buy into the *who—you*.

2. **Choose the Right Platform**

    Don't overcomplicate this. Choose a platform that fits your audience and makes it easy for them to engage. A few powerful options:

- **Circle:** Perfect for building a private, interactive hub. Think Facebook Groups but better design, no distractions, and full control. Paid.

- **Mighty Networks:** Great for courses + community all in one space. Paid.

- **Geneva:** A free, modern community platform with chat, video, events, and more. Especially good for Gen Z and creatives.

- **Discord:** Popular with younger audiences and ideal for real-time chats and niche communities. Free.

- **Facebook Groups:** Still useful if your people are there, but remember—it's a rented platform.

If you're building a faith-based, purpose-driven, or intimate space, platforms like **Circle** and **Mighty Networks** are brilliant for depth over numbers.

3. **Grow Your Email List**

Own your data. Platforms come and go, but your list is yours. Start capturing emails through:

- **Lead magnets** (free eBooks, templates, guides)

- **Waitlists** for upcoming launches

- **Newsletters** that offer genuine encouragement and insight

Top tools to help you build and nurture that list:

- **ConvertKit:** Clean, creator-friendly, and great for automations.

- **MailerLite:** Affordable and simple to use.

- **FloDesk:** Beautiful designs and easy workflows.

- **Beehiiv:** Ideal if you're planning a community-driven newsletter.

4. **Foster Genuine Connection**

Community isn't just content—it's conversation. Create space for people to share their voice:

- Start **threads or prompts** that spark discussion.

- Host **monthly Zoom calls or Q&As.**

- Celebrate member wins and life moments.

- Use tools like **Typeform** or **Google Forms** to get feedback and co-create content with your community.

5. **Monetise with Meaning**

If you're ready to turn your free community into a paid one, do it with intention:

- **Patreon:** Great for creative content and tiered support.

- **Ko-fi:** Accept donations or set up monthly memberships.

- **Kajabi** or **Podia:** Build full-on digital ecosystems with courses, coaching, and memberships.

- **Gumroad:** Sell simple digital products and build a creator base.

But remember: people don't pay for access—they pay for *transformation*. Give them something that shifts them.

Journaling Prompt

Who are you building for—and who are you building with? Reflect on the last five meaningful interactions you had online. Were they surface-level or community-building? How can you create a space (online or offline) where people don't just follow you—but feel like they belong?

9

Build Bridges, Not Walls—Strategic Networking

'The currency of real networking is not greed but generosity'.

— Keith Ferrazzi

'As iron sharpens iron, so one person sharpens another'.

— Proverbs 27:17 (NIV)

You can have the strongest personal brand in the world, but your influence stays capped if no one ever mentions your name in the right rooms. Branding makes people notice you, but networking makes people remember you. And in this next chapter, we shift from being seen to being *sent for*. Because what good is visibility if it doesn't lead to access? What good is being known if no one can trust your name enough to bring you to the table? If your personal brand is your reputation, then your network is your distribution. It carries your name into spaces your feet haven't entered yet. So now, let's talk about how to build authentic, strategic relationships—not for clout, but for *impact*.

People love the idea of being 'self-made'. Many want to have a good come-up story—the person who 'grinded' their way to success with no help, connections, or handouts. It sounds inspiring, but let's be real—that's not how success really works.

Nobody is truly self-made. Everyone who has ever achieved something great has a network of people around them. Even the people who say, 'I got here by myself', had someone vouched for them, taught them, or gave them an opportunity.

The biggest mistake people make in networking is thinking, 'I don't need anyone', or, 'I'll only connect with people when I need something'.

But the truth is, your network is your greatest asset. It's not just about knowing people—it's about being known for the right reasons.

I've had doors open for me not because I was in the room but because someone mentioned my name in a room I had never even entered.

One of my most valuable lessons is never networking *just for the title*. When you limit your interactions to someone's job title, you restrict the bridge you're building. Some of my best relationships came from connecting with people beyond what they do and instead focusing on *who they are*.

I remember when I was planning my wedding, some of my friends were genuinely shocked that certain people were on the guest list. One friend said to me, 'Wait . . . how did you get the CEO of [name withheld] to come to your wedding? That's insane!' I just smiled and said, 'To you, he's a CEO. To me, he's a friend'.

And that's the key—people can feel when you value them beyond their status. That's what creates lasting relationships. Don't chase titles; cultivate trust.

If there's anyone who embodies the power of networking built on consistency, trust, and humility—it's Tyler Perry.

Before becoming a global entertainment mogul, Tyler was overworking in his early days. He performed multiple stage plays in small theatres, often playing multiple characters and selling tickets himself. He wasn't trying to skip steps—he was building with the people around him. He formed relationships with cast members, crew, and his loyal audience. Over time, those people became his advocates.

Most people don't know that his big break didn't come from Hollywood connections—it came from a loyal community that believed in him, bought out his shows, and spread the word like wildfire.

Tyler didn't network up—he networked deep. He built his empire by valuing everyone in the room, not just the ones in the spotlight.

So the key to powerful networking isn't having the largest network—it's having the clearest discernment. Influence isn't about how many people know your name, but about who carries your name with honour. And the people who truly carry your name well aren't always the loudest in the room—they're often the most consistent behind the scenes. We've already explored the difference between chasing visibility and cultivating real connection—between being in rooms and being remembered in rooms. But now, it's time to get practical. Because not every relationship is meant to carry the same weight, and not every connection deserves the same level of access.

Over the years, I've learned that clarity is just as essential as charisma. You can love people and still set boundaries. You can honour people and still manage access. That's why I developed a simple but powerful tool I call the **Traffic Light Network System**—a framework that helps you build relationships with wisdom, intentionality, and peace. Not to impress, but to impact. Not to control, but to *cultivate* meaningful connections that actually align with your destiny.

This system helps you identify:

- Who you're hoping to build with

- Who's in your life but not yet close

- And who's in your corner and should be nurtured deeply

It's about honouring where people are, without forcing connection, and understanding that the goal isn't perfection—it's alignment.

Red Light—Reach with Discernment

These are people who are not in your network yet, but you would like them to be.

They're aspirational connections—people you admire, want to learn from, collaborate with, or grow alongside.

They might be:

- A leader you've been following

- A potential mentor

- A dream client or partner

- Someone you'd love to build with—but haven't met or engaged meaningfully yet

This zone requires respectful pursuit, not pressure. Don't force access. Build consistency, show up with value, and be patient. Timing and alignment are everything.

Yellow Light—Build with Intention

These are people already in your network—but they're more like acquaintances right now. You see potential, but the relationship isn't deep yet.

They might be:

- Colleagues you connect with occasionally

- People you've engaged with online

- Those who admire your work, or whose work you admire

- Individuals where there's energy and alignment, but not yet intimacy

You'd love to move them to green—but that takes time and mutual effort.

Here, the focus is on intentional touch points: check-ins, thoughtful encouragement, shared experiences. Let trust grow naturally.

Side note: I understand not everyone builds relationships the same way. Some people are naturally reserved. Some aren't looking for deep friendships. And that's okay. Not everyone will end up in the green. This isn't about forcing connection—it's about stewarding what's already there with grace and awareness.

Green Light—Go Deep, Go Bold

These are your people. The ones who truly see you.

- They advocate for you without being asked.

- They support you without expecting anything in return.

- They remind you of who you are when you forget.

- They carry your name with honour when you're not in the room.

These aren't just professional contacts—they're **destiny helpers**.

The kind who challenge you with love, speak about you with respect, and celebrate your wins with no hidden agenda. These are the relationships that shape legacy—not just moments. These are the people who pour into you when no one is watching, and expect nothing in return. These are the most important people in your network.

Protect them. Honour them. Make time for them.

Because in a world full of performance and transactions, they represent something sacred: connection without condition.

Discernment helps you understand who's around you—now let's talk about how to build with them. Because once you know who's in your network, the next step is learning how to deepen those connections with purpose. This isn't just about knowing where people stand—it's about knowing how to move with intention. So, let's break down exactly how to build a network that speaks for you.

The Five Key Principles of Strategic Networking

1. Network Across—See the Value in the People Around You

The biggest mistake people make in networking is only looking up. They ignore the people right next to them, chasing after 'big names' instead.

But the truth is, the people next to you right now could be the people who change your life later.

- The person sitting next to you in class could be the future CEO of a company.

- The intern you met last year could be a director in five years.

- The friend who just started their business could be the next prominent entrepreneur.

One of the best examples of this is Issa Rae.

Before she was the creator of Insecure, she made YouTube videos for her friends. She didn't try to chase after Hollywood executives—she built with the people around her. She grew with her team, and when she made it, she brought them with her.

In her words:

'A lot of us don't network across. We're always trying to network up, but there's so much value in building with people at your level and growing together'.

You don't build a network just to get something today— you build a network that grows with you over time.

Think of networking like a bank account: every act of kindness, support, and service is a deposit into someone else's life. You don't give to get—you give to *grow*. This is what I call **network equity**.

Just like financial equity builds over time, so does relational equity. You're planting seeds every time you connect with someone, celebrate their work, or show up for them. Some of those seeds take years to grow. But when the harvest comes, it's always worth it.

So before you ask for anything, ask yourself: *Have I made enough deposits to withdraw this favour?*

2. Position the Introduction: Train People on How to Introduce You

People can only introduce you based on what they understand about you. If you're vague about who you are, your network won't be able to advocate for you properly.

Let's say you're a public speaker. If you just tell people, 'I'm a speaker', what will they say when introducing you?

'This is [your name], they're a speaker'.

That's boring.

But if you say, 'I help leaders communicate their vision with confidence and impact', now people know exactly who you serve and what you do.

When your network knows how to talk about you, they become your marketing team.

Oprah Winfrey is a perfect example of this.

She didn't just introduce herself as 'a talk show host'. She positioned herself as a thought leader, an innovator, and a media mogul.

And because she made it clear who she was, other people introduced her similarly.

Your introduction should do three things:

1. Be clear: People should understand exactly what you do.

2. Be memorable: Make sure your introduction leaves an impression.

3. Be repeatable: If someone introduces you to someone else, would they say the right thing?

Because your introduction isn't just for you—it's for the people who will be introducing you when you're not in the room.

3. Think About Five Ways to Add Value Before You Ask for One Thing

One of the best networking strategies is giving before you ask.

If you approach every connection with, 'What can I get from this?' you'll quickly lose people.

Gary Vaynerchuk, in Jab, Jab, Jab, Right Hook, talks about how giving first builds long-term relationships.

Think about it—when someone constantly supports, promotes, or helps you, don't you naturally want to help them back?

Here are five ways to add value before ever asking for anything:

1. Introduce people to each other—Connecting two people who need each other builds trust.

2. Support their work—Share their business, buy their book, and attend their event.

3. Offer your skill—Help them with something small that showcases your expertise.

4. Celebrate them publicly—Give them a shout-out, endorse them, and mention them.

5. Be a reliable support—Sometimes, adding value is just showing up for people.

The more value you add, the more people want to help you.

4. Network Around the Person You Want to Meet—The Casino Strategy

Let's talk about one of my favourite movies, Casino.

Most people watch it and see a crime movie. But if you watch closely, it's a strategic networking masterclass.

The people in power aren't just powerful on their own. They have an inner circle.

And if you want to get close to someone important, you don't go straight to them.

You build relationships with the people around them.

If you want to meet a CEO, don't just email them— build relationships with their assistant.

If you want to meet a big-time producer, connect with the writers, editors, and crew.

Every influential person has a gatekeeper; the fastest way to gain access is to build trust with the people in their world.

This is exactly how successful people move.

They don't force their way in—they get invited in by the people who already have access.

5. You'll Probably Meet Someone Who Can Change Your Life . . . Are You Ready?

So, let's say you finally meet the person you've been hoping to connect with.

Are you actually ready for the opportunity?

Many people meet life-changing connections, but they fumble because they're unprepared.

Here's how to make sure you're ready:

- Have a clear pitch. If someone asks what you do, you should be able to explain it confidently in 30 seconds.

- Have something to show: a website, a portfolio, or a social media page with your work.

- Have a follow-up strategy. Don't just say, 'Nice to meet you'—find a way to stay in touch.

- Have a way to add value before asking for anything.

Because when the right opportunity comes, you don't want to just take a picture. You want to make a connection that lasts.

In today's world, networking doesn't just happen in conference rooms; it happens in comment sections, DMs, and digital threads. Some of my most powerful collaborations, partnerships, and opportunities started with a single message online—a repost, a thoughtful comment, or a DM that turned into something much more.

But let's be honest: a lot of people get digital networking wrong. They rush the ask, sound robotic, or make it all about them. If you want to build genuine relationships online, you have to lead with value, not with your agenda.

Here's how to do it well—from your first message to your follow-up:

- How to Slide Into DMs (Without Being Weird)

  - **Lead with value:** 'I loved your post on X—it really shifted how I saw Y'.

  - **Be specific:** 'The way you broke down [insert topic] was brilliant'.

  - **Start a dialogue:** 'I'd love to learn more about your work in [industry]'.

  - **Be patient:** Don't jump straight into a pitch.

  - **End with appreciation:** Whether or not they respond, you've left a strong, respectful impression.

Relationships can start with a comment, a repost, or even a prayer. But what truly strengthens the connection is **what you do next**. A good message opens the door. A great follow-up keeps it open.

Let's say they respond—or you meet someone through an event or a mutual connection. Don't just stop at 'nice to meet you.' That's where most people fall off. If you want to turn a moment into momentum, your follow-up needs to be intentional and authentic.

Use this simple five-step formula:

1. **Thank them**—'It was so great connecting with you'.

2. **Recall something specific**—'I loved what you said about X'.

3. **Offer value**—'I'd love to share a resource I think you'd enjoy'.

4. **Suggest the next step**—'Let me know if you'd be open to a quick call, or if I can support your upcoming work'.

5. **Close graciously**—'Either way, wish you the best in all you're building!'

People don't forget thoughtful follow-ups. In a world full of vague messages and surface-level interactions, being clear, kind, and value-driven will make you stand out every single time.

Whether the connection starts in person or online, how you *nurture* it builds trust—and trust is the foundation of every robust network.

At its core, networking isn't about collecting names but cultivating relationships. It's about building bridges that go beyond business cards and social media follows. Everything changes when you stop chasing connections for clout and start nurturing them with consistency, character, and care. Doors open. Rooms make room. And people don't just remember your face—they remember your faithfulness. So, don't wait for the perfect moment to start building your network. Start where you are, with what you have and who you're around. Because the truth is, the right relationships won't just elevate your career—they'll enrich your life. And in the end, it's not just about who you know. It's about who you grow with.

Journaling Prompt

Who in your current circle have you been overlooking that could become a meaningful connection if you nurtured it?

Reflect on how you've been showing up in your relationships—are you depositing into people, or only withdrawing? What bridges do you need to build, and what walls do you need to break down to expand your network with intention and authenticity?

10

Collaboration Is the Cheat Code: Breaking Scarcity and Winning Together

'When "I" is replaced by "We," even "Illness" becomes "Wellness"'.

— Malcolm X

'Two are better than one because they have a good return for their labour:
If either of them falls down, one can help the other up'.

— Ecclesiastes 4:9–10 (NIV)

Networking opens the door, but collaboration builds the house. If networking is about being known, collaboration is about creating something bigger than you. I've already mentioned in the previous chapter that there's a dangerous myth that glorifies doing it alone— that real success means you never needed anyone. But the truth is, nothing lasting is ever built in isolation.

The most impactful movements, messages, and milestones were never solo efforts, but collective ones. The goal isn't just to be in the right rooms; it's to build the kind of relationships that create new rooms altogether. And that's where collaboration comes in.

Society loves telling us that the only way to win is to outwork, outshine, and out-hustle everyone else. But let me be honest with you—that's a lie.

Let me tell you a quick story.

A couple of years ago, I was running myself into the ground. I booked speaking engagements, ran events, mentored, and coached—I did everything myself. And on the surface, it looked like I was winning. I was flying across different countries and speaking at major conferences, and people kept telling me, 'Wow, Hayley, you're killing it!'

But behind the scenes? I was drowning. I had been assigned to build souls but was losing my own. I was missing a lot of opportunities because I was stretched too thin. I remember even being in a time of prayer and feeling like God had spoken back to me and said, 'Hayley, you've become too tired to receive all the opportunities I have lined up for you', which wrecked me.

I didn't realise how I was so focused on doing everything myself that I didn't have the capacity to grow. It wasn't until I started collaborating—building a team, delegating, trusting other people with my vision—that things really shifted.

Some of you are waiting for your breakthrough, but you're resisting the very thing that will take you there: collaborating, trusting others, and understanding that winning is a team effort.

Michael Jordan is one of the greatest basketball players of all time. Period. But do you know what people forget? He didn't win a single championship for the first six years of his career.

Not one.

Why? Because he was trying to do it all by himself. He was dropping crazy points and making insane plays, but he wasn't trusting his team. He believed that he had to take control of the whole game because he was the best.

It wasn't until Phil Jackson introduced the Triangle Offense—a system that forced MJ to play as part of a team—that things started to shift. Jordan had to learn that it wasn't about being the best player; it was about creating the best team.

When did he finally embrace that? Six NBA Championships.

That's the difference between talent and legacy. Legacy isn't built in isolation. Legacy is built through collaboration.

In 2020, I launched my first speaking course. Funny enough, it had the same name as this book: *Speak Up*. I was excited. I believed in it. I told everyone about it. Ten people bought it—and every single one of them asked for a refund. I was embarrassed. I was disappointed. I felt like I missed it.

I tried again . . . masterclasses, digital products, workshops. I was doing all the things, but nothing was consistent. I was visible, but I wasn't building. I was showing up, but I wasn't scaling. I was doing it alone. And I was exhausted.

Then 2023 came—and so did the shift.

I partnered with my incredible husband, Sterling Record. A marketing genius. A systems guy. A visionary in his own right. He didn't just believe in my voice—he knew how to package it, position it, and push it. He became my business partner, and together we rebuilt everything.

He came in and created the systems. He built the funnels. He mapped the journey. And I just focused on the message. What took me years to hit six figures income? Together—we hit six figures in six weeks.

That's the power of alignment. That's what happens when ego steps aside, and wisdom walks in. I had the vision—but he brought the vehicle. I had the gift— but he brought the gears. And together? We finally had momentum.

Some of us are praying for acceleration, but we're rejecting alignment. We want the next level but don't want to let anyone in. But here's what I learned: collaboration isn't a weakness—it's strategy. It's stewardship. It's the difference between building alone, and building something that actually lasts.

God never called us to grind in isolation. He called us to build a partnership.

At the root of resisting partnership is scarcity thinking.

Scarcity says:

- 'If I share my ideas, someone will steal them'.

- 'If I help them, what's left for me?'

- 'If they win, I lose'.

We've been conditioned to believe that success is scarce. That if someone else wins, it somehow takes away from our own potential. We're taught to compete instead of collaborate, from the classroom to the boardroom.

Schools reward individual performance. Job applications ask, 'Why are you the best?' not, 'How well do you build with others?' Even social media turns life into a leaderboard—likes, followers, engagement rates—as if numbers are the only measure of influence.

But let me ask you this: when was the last time you saw someone truly win in isolation?

You might go fast alone, but you go far together.

People who hoard opportunities, gatekeep infor-mation, or operate in silence might seem successful for a season—but eventually, they hit the ceiling. Why? Because real success requires scalability, and you can't scale alone.

Let's take it beyond theory and into the real world.

Kodak once owned 90% of the camera film market. But when digital photography emerged, they clung to the old way. Instead of adapting or partnering with innovators, they resisted change. Their fear of collaboration cost them the future. Today, Kodak is a shadow of what it once was—not because they lacked resources, but because they lacked vision.

BlackBerry? Same story. They dominated the mobile phone industry. However, while Apple and Google were partnering with developers to create an app-based ecosystem, BlackBerry stayed rigid. They refused to collaborate—and they got left behind.

Now, contrast that with companies that embraced abundance.

Apple and Nike didn't compete—they collaborated. The Apple Watch Nike+ was born out of shared strengths: tech meets performance. They could have built separately, but together, they built something that disrupted two industries at once.

Even in entertainment, the principle holds. Beyoncé could've built her own sneaker brand from scratch, but instead, she partnered with Adidas to expand Ivy Park. Not because she needed help, but because she understood that collaboration expands reach, deepens impact, and opens new doors.

Collaboration doesn't take away from your shine—it multiplies it. When we collaborate, we expand opportunities instead of taking them away. There is no cap on success. There is no limit to what can be built when people work together.

This is why we have companies like Apple and Nike partnering. This is why you see Beyoncé working with Adidas, because even the biggest names know that partnership creates power.

Scarcity is fear. Collaboration is freedom. And freedom is where true success lives.

This isn't just about mindset. This is scientifically proven. Humans are social creatures; we are literally designed to thrive in groups.

A study from Harvard University's Department of Psychology found that when people collaborate, the brain releases oxytocin—the chemical that builds trust and strengthens relationships.

Another study from the MIT Human Dynamics Lab found that the most successful teams had

1. Frequent communication—talking and bouncing ideas off each other.

2. High levels of energy and engagement—excited about working together.

3. Open idea sharing—no fear of judgement or rejection.

Do you know what kills teams? Isolation, fear, and competition.

One of my favourite proverbs of all time comes from the continent that raised me:

'If you want to go fast, go alone. If you want to go far, go together'.

Being African, this isn't just a quote—it's a culture. I grew up around people who weren't my blood relatives but still carried titles like 'Aunty' and 'Uncle'. Why? Because they were friends with my mum or dad. And in our community, friendship doesn't end in proximity—it extends into family.

Some of the people who helped raise me weren't tied to me by genetics, but by commitment. Aunties stepped in when my mum was working. Uncles gave guidance when my dad wasn't around. That's the beauty of African collectivism—we understand that raising a child, building a vision, and sustaining a life all require community.

In many Western societies, the opposite is often celebrated. Success is tied to self—what you did, what you built, what you own. The rise of hyper-individualism and consumerism has sold us a lie that being self-made is the ultimate goal.

But what good is building a table if you end up eating at it alone? What good is climbing the ladder if there's no one around to catch you when you fall?

Consumerism tells us to collect.

Individualism tells us to isolate.

But collectivism? It teaches us to carry.

That's why I take so much pride in this African proverb. It reminds me that going alone might feel efficient, but it's often empty. That real legacy isn't built in a vacuum—it's built in community. The moment you stop trying to do everything on your own is the moment you create space for something greater to grow.

In the bible, there's a verse that echoes this beautifully:

'One can chase a thousand, but two can put ten thousand to flight'.
— Deuteronomy 32:30

That's multiplication. That's the power of partnership. That's what happens when you shift from solo building to a shared mission.

And maybe that's the tension we need to confront: the world keeps glorifying independence and quick wins, but true impact takes time—and togetherness. Because while community may not always be the fastest route, it's almost always the most fruitful.

And yet so many of us still find ourselves chasing speed. We want success now. We want an impact immediately. We want influence overnight.

But quick wins don't last. Fast success with no foundation crumbles.

When you go alone, sure, you might move quickly. But when obstacles hit? When life happens? When burnout comes knocking? You realise that you can't sustain the journey on your own.

But when you go together? When you build community, collaboration, and trust? You create something that lasts.

Imagine if Dr Martin Luther King, Jr., tried to do the Civil Rights Movement alone.

Imagine if he said, 'Nah, I don't need anyone else. I'll just march by myself'.

Would change have happened? Absolutely not.

The movement worked because it wasn't just his voice. It was a collective voice. Rosa Parks, John Lewis, Malcolm X, the Freedom Riders, the church leaders, and the students sitting at segregated lunch counters. They moved as one.

One person can spark a fire, but it takes a community to keep it burning.

The phrase 'Black Lives Matter' was first used in 2013 after Trayvon Martin's death. But it wasn't until

2020—when millions of people across the world took to the streets—that the movement shook the world.

What changed?

It wasn't just one person speaking. It was millions. From New York to London, from Paris to Johannesburg—when people came together, the world had no choice but to listen.

That's the power of collaboration.

For years, women tried to speak out against sexual harassment in Hollywood, but their voices were dismissed.

Then came Tarana Burke's #MeToo movement.

When it became a collective voice, when dozens of women came forward against Harvey Weinstein, the industry had no choice but to pay attention.

When multiple survivors came forward against Jeffrey Epstein, the justice system had no choice but to act.

One voice can be ignored.

A chorus of voices cannot.

Collaboration sounds beautiful in theory, but it takes intentionality to live out in practice. Moving from a scarcity mindset to a collaborative one isn't just a shift in language—it's a shift in posture. It requires both self-awareness and strategy.

So, if you're ready to build with others, not just beside them, here are a few practical steps to help you move from isolation to impact.

1. **Check Your Mindset: Are You Operating from Scarcity or Abundance?**

   - Do you hold back on sharing ideas because you're afraid someone will steal them?

   - Do you see other people's success as a threat?

   - Do you hesitate to ask for help because you think it makes you look weak?

If the answer is yes, you're in scarcity mode. And scarcity will always keep you small.

2. **Find Your Collaborators**

The right partnerships will take you further than talent alone ever could.

Ask yourself:

- Who in my network complements my skills?

- Who can I build with instead of competing against?

- Who has strengths in the areas I struggle in?

I remember when I started growing my brand. At first, I was doing everything myself. But when I started collaborating with event organisers, content creators, and business leaders, doors opened faster than I could have ever done alone.

3. **Be a Person of Value**

Collaboration isn't about taking—it's about adding value.

- Share your knowledge.

- Make connections for others.

- Be a giver, not just a taker.

People are drawn to collaborators, not opportunists.

4. **Communicate and Build Trust**

Every successful collaboration is built on clear communication and trust.

- Be honest about what you bring to the table.

- Be transparent about expectations.

- Be willing to listen and compromise.

The best collaborations are built on trust.

5. **Stop Competing and Start Partnering**

Collaboration is the shortcut to success.

Instead of trying to compete with everyone, start asking: 'How can we build together?'

Let me leave you with this:

Some of you are one collaboration away from your next level.

One relationship away from your breakthrough.

One strategic partnership away from changing everything.

But if you stay stuck in scarcity, you'll never experience abundance.

Michael Jordan had to learn teamwork.

Apple partners with other brands.

Movements are built through unity, not isolation.

Some of you are one collaboration away from your next level.

One relationship away from your breakthrough.

One strategic partnership away from changing everything.

It's time to shift. It's time to collaborate. It's time to build together.

If you want to go fast, go alone. But if you want to go far, go together.

So I'll ask you again: Who are you building with?

Journaling Prompt

Who are the people in your life that you've been overlooking, underestimating, or trying to do life without?

What strengths do you bring to a collaboration—and where might you need to let someone else in?

Reflect on a time when a partnership made a vision easier, faster, or better.

Are you truly open to building with others, or are you still holding on to a self-made mindset?

PART IV
The Maths Behind Speaking

11

Your Voice Is Worth the Invoice

'You are not just a brand. You are a business. Treat your voice like the product it is'.

— Marshawn Evans Daniels

'A labourer is worthy of their wages'.

— Luke 10:7 (NKJV)

We've discussed the brand, covered visibility, and dug into the story and soul of your message. But now it's time to have the conversation many avoid—the one about *money*.

What's the point of gaining influence if it never converts into income?

This chapter is about that shift—the sacred transition from being 'seen' to being *sustained*. You weren't created just to inspire—you were created to impact. And in order to sustain that impact long-term, you need to structure your gift so that it doesn't just give, but receives, too.

Let's discuss what it means to get *paid* to speak, coach, create, and *carry* your story—and how to do it without guilt, fear, or compromise.

Part I: The Boldness to Believe You Deserve to Be Paid

I didn't always get paid for my voice. For years, I was pouring into people, showing up fully, staying after events to hug everyone in the room, replying to 50 DMs at a time, and even helping organisations fix their strategy—all for free. And at the time, I thought that was the humble, right thing to do. I thought, 'Well, I'm young. I'm still growing. They're giving me a chance. Let me not ask for anything'.

But behind that 'humble' response was a quiet belief that I wasn't good enough yet to charge.

It wasn't until I realised that my voice was more than inspirational—it was transformational, that I finally shifted my mindset. I realised I wasn't just speaking; I was serving. I wasn't just encouraging; I was equipping. And transformation deserves compensation.

It took me years—and honestly, a lot of healing to get comfortable with being paid, and being paid well. I noticed a pattern as I began to reflect on why it took me so long. So many of us wait to be given permission. We walk around with purpose, but feel like we need external validation before we can profit from it. For some reason, we treat money as if it were the enemy of purpose—especially when you've grown up spiritualising sacrifice, but never strategising sustainability.

One quote that set me free was from *You Are a Badass at Making Money* by Jen Sincero:

'You've got to get over your fear of money and your fear of success. You've got to stop apologising for wanting to be paid'.

That hit me hard. Because I was overdelivering but undercharging. I thought asking to be paid meant I was being selfish or less spiritual. But then I looked at the fruit and realised every time I opened my mouth, something changed. People were getting healed, gaining clarity, and stepping into action. And yet I was walking away with applause, and not a payment.

Then I heard Bishop T.D. Jakes say:

'Your voice is your vehicle—but it's also your value'.

That moment changed everything. My voice had been getting me into rooms, but I hadn't yet assigned value to it. I was waiting for people to pay me without ever making it clear that I charged. That's when I realised people don't devalue you—you undervalue yourself, and they just follow your lead.

But belief is often built in relationships. I'll never forget being 18, and I kept saying, 'No one wants to pay me', even though I was pouring myself out in every room I walked into.

My husband Sterling, who was then only just my friend—who has been a foundational voice in my life for the past decade— he would often remind me of my worth by asking me challenging questions 'what are your prices?'

Back then, I'd say a number I thought was reasonable, and he would look at me and ask, 'But what do you *want* to be paid?'

The truth? I didn't even know. I hadn't allowed myself to dream that far. I had got so used to being grateful for any opportunity that I hadn't created space to explore what I actually deserved.

But he saw something in me. He spoke so much life into me. He reminded me that my value is worth being paid for. His voice has anchored me through seasons of doubt. Sterling has challenged me to scale, to stretch, to stop settling.

When I landed my first ever five-figure speaking engagement, he was actually the first person I told. I cried so hard. Not because I got the gig—but because he had seen the behind-the-scenes journey it took to get there. He believed in me when I didn't yet have the language or the confidence to believe in myself.

Sometimes, people aren't rejecting you—they're just waiting to see if you think you're worth it first.

From there, I realised something crucial: once you believe in your worth, the next step is to structure that belief into systems. Because money isn't the mission—but it *is* a tool.

Too many of us burn out from giving everything away and setting no boundaries. Especially if you're creative. Especially if you're a speaker. Especially if you're a woman. We're out here giving out gold, while others are charging premium prices for plastic.

One of the most liberating books I ever read was *The Big Leap* by Gay Hendricks. He talks about the Zone of Genius—the place where your deepest gifts and greatest impact collide. And he warns against settling for the 'zone of competence' or 'zone of excellence' just because they're comfortable.

That book shook something in me. It taught me that if you stay in places that don't stretch or value you, you will suffocate your purpose just to keep other people comfortable.

You were not born to simply sound good. You were born to shift things. Your voice is not just for a microphone—it's for a movement. And movements need fuel.

And here's the thing—people always find a budget for what they value. I've been in rooms where planners spent £10,000 on catering, £6,000 on décor, and £2,000 on chairs ... and then told me, 'Sorry, we don't really have the budget for a speaker'.

It hit me: it's not about money. It's about perception. And that perception starts with how you see yourself.

Every time you downplay your price when you know what you want to be paid, you water down your worth.

Every time you say, 'I'll do it for free', when you need that payment to make rent, you're chipping away at your own belief.

You're not being greedy when you charge. You're being grounded.

Grounded in the truth that your gift is good soil.

Grounded in the belief that your voice deserves to be resourced.

Grounded in the awareness that you're not just speaking for now—you're speaking for legacy.

Legacy needs leverage.

Part II: Turning Your Voice Into Value—16 Streams and a Framework to Monetise What You Say

Now that your mindset is aligned, let's talk about your model. Knowing your voice has value is only the beginning—building structure around that value is what sustains it. That's where the 'VOICE' framework comes in—a blueprint I created to help you turn your words into wealth.

V—Visibility

I said it before and I'll say it again—you're too broke to not be visible.

Before anyone pays you, they have to see you. Visibility isn't vanity—it's viability. It positions your voice where opportunity can find you. You can't complain about not getting booked if no one knows what you sound like.

Visibility is currency. Start posting value online. Speak for free strategically (not indefinitely).

Join panels. Record yourself giving mini-talks. Build content. Your first paid speaking gig often comes from a free one. But let the free one be a funnel, not a forever thing.

- ✓ Start a podcast or YouTube channel—or do research on which podcasts you can appear on to tap into other people's audience.

- ✓ Create short-form videos that position you as a thought leader (reels, TikToks, shorts).

- ✓ Collaborate with others in your niche.

Remember: People pay who they perceive as present.

Example: Mel Robbins became one of the most sought-after motivational speakers in the world after her short TEDx talk 'How to Stop Screwing Yourself Over' went viral. She wasn't famous beforehand. But that one piece of visibility catapulted her into major stages, book deals, and licensing opportunities.

O—Offer Clarity

Once people see you, they'll ask: 'What exactly do you do?' If you fumble here, you lose the opportunity. Clarity converts. You need to articulate what you offer with precision and power.

What are you actually offering? You must be able to say in one sentence: 'I help [audience] do [result] through [method]'.

You need product clarity. Voice is a skill, yes. But the offer is what you package it in.

I have been able to make 16 different incomes from my one voice. Those different incomes came from understanding my offer and what I bring to the table.

✓ Keynote speaking

✓ Workshop facilitation

✓ 1:1 coaching

✓ Group programmes

✓ Online courses

✓ E-books/audio content

✓ Digital downloads (affirmations, scripts, templates)

✓ Brand voice consultancy

✓ Emceeing/Hosting

✓ Podcast appearances

✓ Voiceovers or narration

✓ Licensing your content

✓ Affiliate partnerships

✓ Community memberships

✓ Masterclasses/webinars

✓ Private training for companies

I've done all 16, from speaking to secondary school students to being flown across the world to speak for Fortune 500s—all from my voice. Once I started creating intentional offers, the game changed.

Start brainstorming all the gifts you have, and all the high-paying skills you have.

Sometimes you don't realise what you carry until you actually write it down, and realise you can get paid for it.

In the list of 16 things I make money from, is there one you think you can do? If so, you deserve to be paid.

I—Income Systems

You've got the visibility, and you've clarified your offer. But here's where most people fall short: the back end, the systems, and the structure. Without them, you stay booked emotionally, but not financially.

This is where many people get stuck: they have no infrastructure. Your voice can get people excited, but your systems keep the money consistent.

- ✓ Use a speaker one-pager—an easy way for clients to read about you and what you offer

- ✓ Create a Stripe/PayPal/Bank transfer system if you're looking to do coaching, courses, or release online products

- ✓ Use Calendly for booking—this saves you time going back and forth between clients

- ✓ Build a simple website or landing page—make sure you have a booking form on there so it's easy for anyone to book you to speak or to work with you

- ✓ Use AI to help you Draft email templates for pitching and following up

- ✓ Set up Zoom or other delivery tools for coaching/courses

No system? No scale.

C—Credibility+Case Studies

Before we talk about credibility, let me tell you something about the art of scaling, you have to do it incrementally. You can't just jump from £50 to £500. You have to build credibility at the £50 level, and once you have enough evidence you can give value for that price, you can raise it, maybe to £200.

Establishing yourself overtime is key to scaling—you cannot rush greatness. You must be willing to scale steadily, so no one can call you a fraud.

The key is to ALWAYS charge your worth, but over-deliver on value.

Just remember, people don't just pay because you're talented—they pay because you're trusted. And trust is built through consistency and proof.

Build a portfolio of wins. Collect testimonials. Capture photos and videos when you speak. Write case studies. If you helped someone go from insecure to impactful—document it.

✓ Ask every client for a testimonial

✓ Post 'before and after' results

✓ Share transformation stories of those you've helped

✓ Let your impact speak before your invoice does

Example: Rachel Hollis went from blogger to bestselling author and international speaker because she consistently showed her impact. She shared client wins, audience responses, and behind-the-scenes content, building trust and credibility, and leading to sold-out events and media features.

E—Expansion

Once the foundations are in place, don't stop at one stream. Expansion isn't just about doing more—it's about doing what aligns and scales. Multiplying impact without multiplying burnout.

Once you've built one stream, don't stop there.

Explore expanding through:

✓ Licensing your content to schools or companies

✓ Turning a keynote into a course

✓ Offering a membership community

✓ Selling physical, digital products

✓ Partnering with brands for campaigns

So now you've got the mindset, the framework, and the flow. But let's bring it home with action. You don't need a miracle to start, but you do need a move.

Here are 10 practical things you can do *this month* to start monetising your voice:

1. Create a speaker one-pager. List your topics, audience types, and previous engagements.

2. Pitch to 10 podcasts. Share your story. Plug your offer.

3. Design a one-hour online masterclass. Charge £20–£50, and promote it across social media.

4. Start posting 3–4 videos a week, sharing your expertise. Use CTAs in the caption (Calls to Action). Either encourage people to DM you if they want you to speak at their event, or to share this with a friend who may be interested in your content

5. Build a digital product—a workbook, affirmation audio, or a guide.

6. Offer 1:1 voice coaching or storytelling sessions. Use Calendly to automate.

7. Send value-based DMs or emails to 10 companies or schools. 'I'd love to serve your staff/students with a talk on X'.

8. Collect video testimonials from past clients or events. Post them weekly.

9. Write a short e-book or PDF guide. Use Gumroad or stanstore to sell.

10. Ask past clients for referrals. Most people don't follow up. Do it!

And here's the final thing I'll say—you can't be scared to be paid.

You are not a fraud. You're just early in your income journey. But that voice in your chest? That story you carry? That message burning inside you?

It's worth more than applause. It's worth the invoice.

Stop shrinking. Stop stalling. And stop showing up for exposure when it's time to show up for exchange.

You're not asking to be paid for your presence. You're asking to be paid for your power.

So go. Build. Speak. Sell. And know that you are not just a speaker; you are a solution.

And solutions deserve compensation.

Journaling Prompt

What limiting beliefs do I hold about being paid for my gift? Where did they come from and am I ready to rewrite that story?

12

Beyond Borders: Speaking and Scaling Internationally

'Your dreams in Africa are just as valid in America. Your purpose does not change because your geography does'.

— Dr Tererai Trent

'Go into all the world and preach the gospel to all creation'.

— Mark 16:15 (NIV)

We ended the last chapter by establishing that your voice is worth the invoice. But now, let's take that same voice and stretch its wings. Because when you've mastered value locally, the next natural step is vision globally. Going from getting paid to going global isn't about ego, but expansion. In this chapter, we will unpack what moving from being recognised in rooms to being requested in regions looks like. This is about a legacy that crosses borders.

I never planned to speak across continents. Honestly, I just wanted to help people, to give voice to the things that so many of us were feeling but didn't know how to say out loud. I started in school halls and community centres, speaking to whoever would listen—sometimes five people, sometimes fifty. I was just passionate about people, healing, purpose, and truth. And over time, I realised something powerful: purpose doesn't have a postcode.

What started as a passion to speak up slowly became a passport to the world.

I've now had the honour of speaking across the United Kingdom, Europe, Africa, the United States, and the Middle East. From boardrooms in London to leadership forums in Dubai, from youth summits in New York to schools in Accra—each country, each culture, and each stage taught me something new about what it means to carry a message that transcends borders.

But let me be honest: going global isn't just about flights and flags. It's not about ticking off destinations or stacking your LinkedIn bio. It's about depth, not just distance. It's about resonance, not just reach. And above all—it's about responsibility. Because when people trust you with a microphone, what they're giving you is their time, mind, and sometimes even heart.

And that's not something to take lightly.

As you begin to consider what it truly means to influence across nations, you'll find that intentionality is the thread that holds impact together.

One thing I've learned is that influence without intentionality becomes noise. When you start growing a platform across cultures and countries, your words land differently in different rooms. In one space, your accent may be celebrated. In another, misunderstood. In some spaces, being direct is seen as confident—in others, it can be rude. You've got to learn the language of the room, and I don't just mean linguistics. I mean tone, sensitivity, and presence.

But the truth is that if your message is rooted in authenticity, it will always find a way to connect.

I remember the first time I spoke in Uganda. After the session, a young woman approached me and said, 'You reminded me of who I was before the world tried to water me down'. That sentence wrecked me. At that moment, I realised that my voice had become a mirror for her breakthrough. And I hadn't even known her name.

That's when I knew that speaking isn't about being impressive. It's about being impactful.

And I'm not alone in that revelation. Some of the most powerful examples of international influence have come from people I know personally.

My dear friend Vee Kativhu is such a powerful example of what it looks like to be a global voice. An Oxford and Harvard graduate, yes—but beyond the accolades, she has used her story to empower young girls worldwide to dream bigger, aim higher, and believe deeper. Whether speaking at the UN or mentoring girls through her platform, Empowered by Vee, she's shown that when you own your story, your story will take you places you never imagined.

Then there's my girls, Courtney and Renee—the duo behind 'To My Sisters', the global podcast that's gone from voice notes to millions of downloads across continents. They built something real, raw, and revolutionary. They didn't wait for a big brand to back them. They built their own table and invited the world to sit at it. Whether hosting sold-out live shows or nurturing their sisterhood community online, they've proved that consistent, vulnerable conversations can cross oceans.

These women are proof that going global isn't about going viral. It's about being valuable.

So if you're wondering what it takes to start walking in your own global assignment, let me share the principles that have shaped my journey.

Don't chase global if you're still vague about your local. Don't chase the global if you're not committed to the local. We get so caught up in the idea of being seen by the world that we overlook the stage right in front of us. Your message must make sense at home before it can make noise abroad. Excellence echoes—but only if it's built on something real. Depth, consistency, integrity.

I didn't start on stages with bright lights and polished panels. I started in East London—specifically in the borough of Newham. Speaking in places where the mic didn't work, the heating barely did, and the crowd wasn't always paying attention. I spoke in café corners, hired out halls with my money, and even returned to my old secondary school just to pour back in. I wasn't doing it for recognition—I was doing it because I knew that if I can't give back to the block that built me, I've got no business trying to bless the world.

That was my training ground. That was where God tested my posture before He gave me a platform. And trust me—God is watching how you handle the 'few' before He releases the 'many'. Scripture says in Matthew 25:21, 'Well done, good and faithful servant. You have been faithful with a few things; I will put you in charge of many things'. That's not just a nice verse—it's a principle. God doesn't promote ambition; He promotes stewardship. He doesn't reward platform-chasers; he elevates those who serve with purity.

If you're sloppy with your local, why would He trust you with the global?

Some of us despise our early days because they don't match our vision boards. But the local stage isn't less than—it's where you're built. It's where God forges your character, your competence, and your capacity. If I couldn't make it make sense to a group of teenagers in Newham, how could I expect to move an audience in Cape Town or Chicago?

Before you scale your voice, steward it.

Travelling doesn't make you global—connecting does. It's not just about touching down in a country, but tuning into the culture. I remember when I was first invited to speak in the Middle East. Before I packed a suitcase, I reached out to people in my network who were already living there—asking questions, listening deeply, and learning everything I could. I wanted to understand business etiquette, communication norms, and how respect is expressed differently. I didn't try to impress—I showed up willing to learn.

Most people don't know that I travelled to Dubai alone at least four times before I ever booked a paid speaking engagement there. No client, no cheque—just praying, sowing, and honouring the land. No ulterior motives. I invested in the culture before I expected it to invest in me. Because how can you expect to be received in a place you've never tried to understand? That heart posture—of humility, honour, and preparation—opened doors no pitch ever could.

Entitlement will make you miss your moment. Thinking you deserve opportunities you're not willing to work for is not only dangerous but delusional. The truth is, impact doesn't come to the entitled; it comes to the equipped. And equipping yourself starts with doing the quiet, humble, behind-the-scenes work nobody claps for—but Heaven sees.

Before I ever stepped on an international stage, my content did.

One day, someone messaged me from the United States and said, 'I watched your talk on YouTube, and it changed my life'. I didn't even know the video was still circulating. That one video led to a Zoom call, which led to a referral, which led to a speaking gig.

Social media isn't just for visibility—it's for velocity. The right video, reel, post, or podcast clip can cross borders in seconds. You're one post away from someone in Ghana, Canada, or Dubai discovering your voice. This is why it's so important to show up with intention. Use your online presence wisely. Post with purpose. Show up excellently—even if you're creating content from your bedroom. You don't need a flight to be global. You need to be found faithful.

And it wasn't just content that gave me global reach—it was community.

Sometimes, God won't just give you a platform—He'll give you people. Relationships that carry rooms you haven't even stepped into yet. And you honour those relationships by showing up with consistency, humility, and excellence.

Visibility isn't just about being seen by the world—it's about being planted in the right soil, with the right voices, and posture. Because when you do that? The rooms will come. The referrals will come. The stages will come.

And they'll find you already ready.

Your voice might open the door, but your values keep it open.

I've had people book me—not because of my pitch, but because they watched how I carried myself when no one clapped. They saw how I honoured the volunteers; how I thanked the media team; how I showed up early, prepared, and low-maintenance; how I stayed behind after speaking engagements—not rushing out, but staying present. Taking time to speak with attendees, hear their stories, pray, and remind them that they were seen. Because for me, the real impact doesn't just happen on the stage—it happens in the moments after.

Reputation travels faster than you do. People will talk about you in rooms you've never stepped foot in. And when they do, what will they say?

Some of the opportunities I've been presented with weren't just because of my voice, but my values. I've been invited to speak because I'm bold about my faith, because I don't water it down to be palatable. I've had doors open because I'm visibly committed to my marriage. I don't hide that I'm family-oriented, or that I carry my relationship with care. In a world where many are afraid to stand for something, people notice when you do—and they remember how you live, not just what you say.

People don't just watch your moves—they watch your commitments. They watch your consistency. They pay attention to how you treat people when no one's watching, honouring what matters to you, and carrying yourself in rooms that require grace more than glamour.

Your values are your true global currency. Let integrity be your passport. Because influence not anchored in character is just noise—I'd rather be known for what I stood for than just what I said.

It's not just about being bold—it's about being clear. I've seen confident speakers own the stage but lose the audience because they didn't take the time to connect. Real communication isn't about sounding impressive. It's about making people feel understood.

I'll never forget a time I was speaking at a college in North London. The audience was beautifully diverse— students from all over the world. I started speaking with my usual rhythm and flow, but I could sense something was off. They weren't engaged. Some looked lost. And that's when it hit me: just because we were in the United Kingdom didn't mean everyone in the room was fluent in English.

I had assumed instead of understanding.

So I paused, slowed down, swapped out idioms and metaphors, and made space for questions. I adapted—not because I didn't know my content, but because I cared more about their experience than my performance.

That day changed everything. It taught me that communication isn't about you—it's about them. You're not there to deliver a monologue. You're there to build a moment of connection.

It doesn't matter how well you said it if they don't get it.

Going global isn't about ego—it's about obedience. For me, speaking has never been about popularity. It's always been about purpose. Every stage, every city, every seat is an assignment. I don't just go places to speak—I go to serve. To sow. To shift atmospheres.

When I look back on the countries I've spoken in, it's not the lights or the logistics I remember—it's the lives. The girl in Uganda had tears in her eyes. The student in East London who said, 'I didn't know people like you existed'. The woman in Atlanta who waited until the end just to say, 'You put words to what I've been carrying in silence'. That's what this is about. Not just visibility—but impact. It's not just going viral—but going deep.

So, if you dream of going global, ask yourself: Can I be trusted with the weight of influence? Can I carry my voice with humility, consistency, and honour?

Because this is bigger than content—it's calling. Bigger than reach—it's responsibility. 'And who knows but that you have come to your royal position for such a time as this?' (Esther 4:14). Maybe you weren't just born to speak—but to liberate a generation. Maybe your boldness will break cycles. Maybe your obedience will shift atmospheres across nations.

The world isn't just waiting to hear your voice—it's depending on it. So don't just aim to be heard—aim to be helpful. Don't just cross borders—build bridges.

Your voice matters. And maybe, just maybe; you were born for such a time as this.

Journaling Prompt

What part of my voice, message, or mission have I been keeping local out of fear or hesitation? How would I prepare myself—spiritually, practically, and professionally—to go global?

PART V

The Future
of Speaking

———

13

Rejection Is Redirection

'The stone the builders rejected has become the cornerstone'.

— Psalm 118:22 (NIV)

'Rejection can be God's way of saying: I've got something better'.

— Tyler Perry

They won't always clap.

They won't always get it.

They won't always say yes.

And that's okay.

If you're going to build a personal brand, grow in your calling, or walk in purpose—criticism and rejection are not just likely. They're guaranteed. You can't pray your way around them. You can't outwork your way past them. You have to learn how to outgrow them.

But let's be honest. Rejection hurts. It hits in the gut, especially when you've placed your hope, heart, or identity in something or someone. I used to think if I worked hard enough, I could avoid rejection. If I was nice enough, humble enough, or talented enough, I could dodge criticism. But the truth is—even Jesus was rejected in His hometown. And He was literally perfect.

When I first pursued speaking, my first rejection was from my mum.

I love my mum deeply. She's my queen. She's sacrificed so much for me to have the life I live. But when I first told her I wanted to become a speaker ... she wasn't exactly clapping for it. Not because she didn't believe in me, but because she didn't understand it. In her world, 'speaker' wasn't a real job—it sounded like a distraction, a phase, or something that couldn't build a secure future.

'You want to talk for a living?' she said.

'You need to focus on school, not this speaking thing you want to do'.

I remember feeling the sting of that. I wasn't angry—I was just hurt. I had a fire in me, but I didn't know how to explain it to someone who had never seen that kind of path work. And that's the thing—people can't always see what you've been called to walk out.

Consist, and they will see.

That is consistency.

I just stayed focused. I didn't chase validation—I chased vision. And now, by God's grace, my mum is also enjoying the fruits of my labour. I've been able to fly her out, upgrade her flights to business multiple times—not out of obligation, but as a small thank-you for everything she's done for me.

Her 'no' didn't stop me—it shaped me.

Sometimes, no is exactly what you need.

At 18, I found a mentor I admired. I thought he would open doors, but instead, he tried to shut mine.

'Hayley, I just don't think anyone will want to hear from a Black woman like you'.

Those words didn't just sting. They hit a place in me that was already tender. Growing up without a father, I craved a father's voice—that sense of approval, affirmation, and direction. And in that moment, this mentor's words didn't just discourage me—they nearly crushed me.

But I had to remind myself: he didn't call me—God did.

I couldn't afford to find my identity in someone else's opinion, no matter how respected they were. I had to anchor myself in what God had already said about me: 'I praise you because I am fearfully and wonderfully made; your works are wonderful, I know that full well' (Psalm 139:14, NIV).

And the truth is, when you're deeply rooted in your God-given identity, rejection doesn't shake you; it sharpens you. It doesn't derail you; it directs you.

The more I aligned myself with what God said, the less weight I gave to what people thought.

Years later, that same man told me he was proud of me. That he respected my consistency. And I didn't have to prove anything; I just had to keep planting and keep showing up. Sometimes, your boldness will silence the voice of doubt—not by shouting but by showing.

There was a brand I adored. I had dreamed about speaking at their event. I followed them, engaged with them, prayed about it—and when I finally reached out, the answer was no.

It wasn't a rude no—but it was final. 'Not right now'. I took away their feedback and improved. It got to a point where they kept hearing about me, and other clients and prospects were now referring me and even asking them, 'Why haven't you booked Hayley to speak at your conferences?'

Fast forward four years later—that same brand reached out to me. Not just to speak at their event, but to consult with them long-term on personal branding and visibility.

And in that moment, I had a quiet laugh with God. Because He knew what I didn't.

I thought I was ready—but I wasn't.

I thought it was rejection—but it was refinement.

There's something I always say:

'I would rather God deal with me in private than let me embarrass myself in public'.

Sometimes, His 'not yet' is actually His protection. He sees what's ahead—and sometimes we're praying for things that our character hasn't caught up to carry yet.

Before we even get into the framework, let me be honest—I didn't always take criticism well. Especially in the early days of my speaking journey, I equated feedback with failure. But what I've learned over the years is this: criticism isn't always an attack; sometimes it's a call to personal accountability.

One of the greatest leadership principles I've learned from John Maxwell is from *The 21 Irrefutable Laws of Leadership*—specifically, The Law of the Mirror, which teaches that you must see value in yourself to add value to others. But part of that process means being honest with what needs work. Accountability is a mark of maturity.

Some of the best feedback I've received came from people who told me the truth—not to hurt me, but to help me. And while it stung in the moment, it sharpened me for the future. John Maxwell often says, 'Everything rises and falls on leadership'. And if I'm going to lead, I have to be willing to be led—even if that leadership comes in the form of tough love, or constructive critique.

Take Bukayo Saka, for example. After missing a crucial penalty in the UEFA Euro 2020 final, he faced an overwhelming wave of criticism and even racial abuse. At just 19 years old, the pressure could have broken him—but instead, he used it as fuel. He returned to training, strengthened his mindset, and delivered one of his best seasons with Arsenal, becoming a standout player for both club and country. Saka didn't shy away from the pain of public failure; he embraced it, learned from it, and turned it into purpose. His maturity and grace under pressure have inspired millions—proving that sometimes, what breaks you publicly is the very thing that builds you privately.

Sometimes, criticism doesn't expose your weakness—it reveals your edge. You just have to be mature enough to discern the difference.

Criticism is a mirror, not a definition.

And how you handle it determines if it moulds you, or messes with you.

Let's Break It Down with a Framework I Call R.E.A.L.

R—Reflect

Before reacting, pause. Ask yourself: Is there any truth in this?

Not everything needs a response. Not every comment is an attack. Growth starts when we listen for what's useful and drop what's not.

Dr Tasha Eurich, an organisational psychologist, found that only about 10–15% of people are truly self-aware. Reflecting before reacting is one of the key habits of emotionally intelligent people—it gives you power over your narrative, not just your emotions. Growth starts when we listen for what's useful, and drop what's not.

E—Evaluate the Source

Not all criticism is created equal. You shouldn't take feedback from people who aren't even walking where you're heading. Are they wise? Are they invested in your growth? Or are they just projecting their own pain?

As Morgan Freeman once said, 'Never take criticism from someone you wouldn't go to for advice'. It's a reminder that credibility matters. If someone's voice hasn't been assigned to your vision, their criticism shouldn't be either. Evaluate the fruit before you accept the feedback.

A—Align with Your Values

Let the critique push you closer to who you really are, not who they think you should be. When your values are clear, your confidence becomes unshakeable—even when voices around you are loud.

According to research published in the *Journal of Personality and Social Psychology*, people who stay grounded in personal values are significantly more resilient under pressure. That alignment builds the inner strength necessary to withstand external doubt.

L—Let It Fuel You

Use it. Let it make you better, sharper, bolder. Critics may give commentary, but they rarely step in the ring. Don't let the voice in the cheap seats distract you from your God-given stage.

When Serena Williams was told early on that her style was 'too aggressive' and that she would never dominate the sport, she let the critique push her to train harder. The result? Twenty-three Grand Slam titles. She didn't let criticism shut her down—she let it level her up.

History is full of legends who were told 'no':

Walt Disney was fired by a newspaper editor who said he 'lacked imagination and had no good ideas'. He went on to face multiple bankruptcies before finally launching Disneyland—a vision many called foolish at the time.

Today, Disney is one of the most influential brands in the world.

Brian Chesky, co-founder of Airbnb, was rejected by multiple investors who couldn't understand the idea of strangers sleeping in each other's homes. In 2008, after facing rejections from seven major venture capital firms, he and his co-founders created limited-edition cereal boxes to fund the company.

Today, Airbnb is a multi-billion dollar platform that transformed the travel industry—all because he refused to let rejection be the final chapter.

Colonel Harland Sanders had his chicken recipe rejected over 1,000 times before someone finally said yes. He started KFC in his 60s—proving it's never too late and that rejection doesn't have to be the final word.

Adele was rejected by multiple record labels early in her career. One executive even told her she didn't have the 'look' to sell records. But she stayed true to her sound and her story—and today, she's one of the best-selling music artists of all time, with a voice that has broken records and touched hearts across the globe.

What if they stopped because of someone else's opinion?

What if you do?

Rejection will come. Criticism will come. But don't let it stop you from becoming who you're capable of being.

Sometimes you're overlooked not because you're not good enough, but because you're being positioned for something greater. Sometimes the door closes not because you weren't capable, but because the room wasn't aligned with your purpose. Rejection isn't always the end—sometimes, it's the spark that unlocks your evolution.

Rejection is where resilience is built. The greatest leaders, innovators, and creatives didn't avoid it—they used it. They didn't let one 'no' cancel their entire future. They let it teach them, stretch them, and prepare them for something bigger.

So if you're in a season of silence—don't resent it. Let it develop you. Let it sharpen your focus. Let it remind you that greatness is often formed in the quiet.

You don't need everyone to understand you. You just need the grit to keep showing up. Because the right doors? They don't need forcing. They open when you're the version of you that's ready to handle what's behind them.

And when that moment comes—when the yes finally finds you—you'll realise it wasn't luck. It was preparation, persistence, and patience. Every 'no' sharpened you. Every closed door made you more resourceful. And now, you're not just walking into rooms—you're owning your space in them.

Let them talk. Let the doors close. Let it refine you.

Just don't let it define you.

Reflection Questions

What rejections have I taken personally that were actually divine redirections?

Who are the voices I've been giving weight to that God never told me to follow?

What skills or habits is God asking me to build in the waiting?

Am I looking for validation from the crowd, or confirmation from God?

Journaling Prompt

Write about a moment in your life when a 'no' felt devastating at the time but ended up being one of the biggest blessings in disguise. What did you learn? How did you grow?

What rejections have I taken personally that were actually divine redirections?

Who are the voices I've been giving weight to that God never told me to follow?

What skills or habits is God asking me to build in the waiting?

Am I looking for validation from the crowd, or confirmation from God?

Affirmation

I will not fear rejection, because I know who called me. Every 'no' is working together for my good. I am growing, I am refining, and I will walk through the doors that are meant for me—in God's timing, not mine.

14

A New Record

'Don't aspire to make a living; aspire to make a difference'.

— Denzel Washington

'Let your light shine before others, that they may see your good deeds and glorify your Father in heaven'.

— Matthew 5:16 (NIV)

This is the final chapter.

And not just of this book—but of an old mindset, an old way of living, an old narrative that told you your voice didn't matter or your impact was insignificant. This chapter is more than an ending—it's a beginning. A divine reminder that you were never just meant to read stories of transformation and Legacy—you were called to live them. If you've made it this far, I need you to know something: you're not here by accident. You've been entrusted with influence. And now, you are responsible for leaving your Record—not just for applause, but for assignment. Not for validation, but for generations.

As we close these pages together, I pray something inside you opens wider.

In 2022, I married my incredible husband, Sterling Record. I still smile thinking about how I used to tease him, even years before we got married, that his future wife would be blessed to have his last name. It was 2016 when we first met, and back then, I had no idea I'd be the one to carry that name. But God—in His divine orchestration—had a beautiful plan. And now, here I am, proudly bearing the name Record.

I remember the first time I looked up the meaning of the word record. It means 'to set down in writing or some other permanent form for later reference', but it also has another definition that speaks volumes—a record is the best performance or most remarkable achievement in a particular activity. A record is a marker. A benchmark. A standard that redefines what is possible. When I got married, I felt something shift in me. My life was no longer just about what I could build for myself; it was about what I would build for future generations.

Marriage marked a turning point. It wasn't just a union of two people; it was a merger of destiny. I realised that the trajectory of my life had changed. I was no longer running just for myself—I was running for something bigger than me, creating A NEW RECORD. The Bible tells us that in the last days, people will become lovers of themselves, selfish, self-absorbed, and disconnected from the bigger picture. But Legacy refuses to live like that. Legacy is the decision to live for more than yourself.

And here's the thing: 'If you're too big to serve, you're too small to lead' (John C. Maxwell). True Legacy isn't rooted in your leadership but in your servanthood.

Maxwell often reminds us, 'The true measure of leadership is influence—nothing more, nothing less'. The most significant influence comes not from being above others but from being willing to get beneath them to lift them up. There is no greater model of this than Jesus Christ—the one who knelt to wash His disciples' feet, healed the sick, fed the hungry, forgave the sinner, and ultimately laid down His life for all. He didn't use His power to dominate; He used it to redeem. Jesus redefined leadership not by status but by sacrifice.

And even today, we see glimpses of that same heart in modern leaders like Jacinda Ardern, former New Zealand prime minister. She led her nation through tragedy and crisis with empathy, transparency, and strength. Whether comforting grieving families after the Christchurch mosque shootings or prioritising well-being over political gain, she showed the world that kindness and competence coexist, and that serving your people will always speak louder than ruling over them.

God did not place you on this earth just so you could uncover all your hidden talents and treasures. That's part of the assignment—yes. But the greater call? It's to help others discover what they carry, too. The legacy lives in the ripple effect. It lives in the impact you make, not just in stages or success, but in lives changed and seeds planted.

And this isn't just about business or ministry—it's about daily life. Legacy is the kindness you show when no one's watching. It's the courage to speak the truth even when it's inconvenient. It's the resilience to keep going when quitting looks easier. It's about becoming the kind of person you want your children, students, mentees, or team to model after. Legacy starts with your character.

Legacy is not fame. It's not virality. It's not a platform or a following. Legacy is what remains when you're no longer in the room. It's the stories people tell about how you made them feel. It's the fingerprints you leave on people's hearts. It's the values, the impact, and the culture you cultivate that outlives you.

Take Chadwick Boseman.

When the world first saw him on-screen as King T'Challa in Black Panther, we witnessed something more than just another blockbuster movie. We saw a cultural moment. A man walking in divine purpose. A portrayal of Black royalty, leadership, and excellence that redefined what it meant to be a hero—not just in fantasy, but in real life.

But what most people didn't know was that Chadwick was fighting a private battle with cancer. While the world praised him for his strength, talent, and grace, he was quietly enduring chemotherapy, surgeries, and immense physical pain—all while still showing up, performing at the highest level, and encouraging others. He chose to stay silent about his illness, not out of pride but out of purpose.

He didn't want sympathy to overshadow the message. He wasn't building a brand; he was building a legacy.

He used his platform not just for personal gain, but for generational impact. He was deeply intentional about the roles he chose, portraying real-life heroes like Jackie Robinson, Thurgood Marshall, and James Brown. Each character carries historical and cultural weight. Each role served a greater vision—to remind Black people of their worth, brilliance, and resilience.

In one of his final public speeches, Chadwick said:

> 'When God has something for you, it doesn't matter who stands against it. God will move someone who's holding you back away from a door and put someone there who will open it for you if it's meant for you'.

That wasn't just a quote; that was a revelation. Chadwick understood something deeply spiritual: Legacy is not about being seen; it's about being sent. He lived like a man who knew his time was limited, and he maximised it. He reminded us that purpose isn't about duration; it's about depth. You can live 80 years and leave no impact, or you can live 43 like Chadwick and shake the world.

His Legacy is etched in more than just movies. It's in how he carried himself—with quiet confidence, humility, reverence, and deep awareness of the responsibility in his life. He didn't use his influence to chase attention; he used it to spark imagination and healing.

And that's what Legacy really is: choosing to be impactful rather than impressive.

Chadwick Boseman reminded the world that greatness doesn't always have to be loud. Sometimes it's dignified. Sometimes it's hidden. Sometimes it's fighting battles no one sees while still making others feel seen.

That kind of Legacy? It's eternal.

One of the greatest enemies of Legacy is complacency. Legacy builders don't settle. They're not satisfied with just enough. They're driven by vision, conviction, and eternity.

Complacency whispers, 'You've done enough', but Legacy declares, 'There's still more to do'. It tells you to play it safe, to coast, to assume that once you've reached a certain milestone, the work is finished. But Legacy knows better. Legacy understands that your assignment doesn't end when you're comfortable—it ends when your impact is complete.

There's a holy discomfort that keeps legacy builders awake at night—not out of anxiety, but out of assignment. They know there are still lives to impact, systems to challenge, and ceilings to break. They're not content with being average or staying the same. They stretch themselves not for status, but for service.

Don't let comfort rob you of your calling. Don't confuse a pause for a permanent stop. Some of the greatest moves of God in history came from people who refused to settle. Abraham left everything. Ruth stayed loyal when others left. Esther risked her life for a greater cause. Their stories became Legacy because they didn't fold in the face of complacency—they rose.

Let me tell you a story—a simple fable, but a powerful one:

There was once a village plagued by drought. The elders asked everyone to dig wells in anticipation of rain. One young man began digging passionately. After digging six feet, he found nothing. Discouraged, he moved a few feet over and started again. Six feet deep—still nothing. He repeated this over and over, digging shallow holes across the land, but never finding water. Meanwhile, another young woman chose a single spot and kept digging. It was hard, dry, discouraging. But she stayed committed. After digging deep enough, she struck water. Her well overflowed and nourished the entire village. The first man had many attempts—but no results. The second had depth—and her perseverance created Legacy.

That story is a mirror for us. Complacency keeps you surface-level. Legacy demands that you dig deep.

And here's an anecdote from real life:

A friend of mine once had a dream to start a nonprofit for young women. She was passionate, full of ideas, and even raised money. But the moment things got hard— when doors closed, when people said no when it felt lonely—she stopped. Years later, someone else launched a similar vision, and it took off. Watching someone else fulfil the very thing you were called to do can be heartbreaking—but it's a reminder: vision without perseverance is a missed opportunity.

Complacency will convince you to put things off until next year, next season, or 'when it's perfect'. But Legacy requires you to move now. Even if it's messy. Even if you're unsure. Even if it's small beginnings.

Never settle for what's easy when what's eternal is still on the table.

We live in a generation that often prioritises promises over processes, and destinations over journeys. But here's the truth: the journey establishes you, and the process shapes you. You cannot have promises without processes because the process keeps you grounded in your promise.

It is through the process that you develop grit, perseverance, discipline, character—the very things necessary for long-term success.

I often say that if you want success in the long run, you must be willing to endure the long run. I recently shared on a podcast that champions are not made in the ring; they are seen in the ring. The process that allows them to win tournaments and championships is not visible. It is gritty and challenging.

Reflecting on my journey, I realise I won't share everything online—not because I'm hiding anything, but because some parts of the journey are sacred. Some seasons are silent, so God can shape you without distraction. However, when you've overcome, sharing becomes important so others can see what's possible.

Understanding the power of the process, and not shying away from it, is crucial. When it comes to success, you must be willing to put in the work.

Think about Usain Bolt. He trained for over ten years to run for just ten seconds. The world record for the hundred metres is under ten seconds—and this man dedicated a decade to achieve that life-changing moment.

But Usain's Legacy isn't just about speed. It's about discipline, consistency, and character. It's about someone who stayed committed even when no one was watching. His confidence on the track came from years of unseen repetition. His greatness wasn't just in what he did but how he did it—with joy, humility, and excellence.

He made history, yes. But he also made belief possible for others. Young runners across the globe now know what's achievable because he showed them. His Legacy is not just a world record—it's a world impact. It's a reminder that when you prepare in private, you can perform in public. When you honour the process, you create a platform that speaks louder than any words.

Even off the track, Usain has continued to invest in the next generation—mentoring, inspiring, and building initiatives that focus on youth development, especially in his home country of Jamaica. His Legacy extends beyond medals; it's in the mindsets he's helped reshape. He reminds us all that Legacy is not about the moment of victory, but about the journey of endurance and excellence that led to it.

So many people desire ten seconds of fame, but are unwilling to invest ten years of hard work, prayer, and perseverance.

Teaching yourself delayed gratification is vital. Understanding that not everything happens instantly will help you realise that the same day you plant a seed is not the same day you can harvest. Harvesting takes time. Anyone familiar with agriculture knows that it takes consistent nurturing.

When you think of your life as a 'record', the question becomes: what mark are you setting? What standard are you establishing? What will others remember?

Most people don't consider this, but someone will likely need to summarise it in a eulogy at the end of your life. Think about that. A few minutes to speak about a lifetime. What will be said about you when you're no longer here? Will they struggle to find words, or will your life speak for itself?

The truth is—you get the chance to write that eulogy now. With every decision you make, every person you serve, every seed you plant—you are writing the summary of your life. The question is: what do you want it to say?

There's no greater example of a legacy than Jesus Christ of Nazareth. He walked the earth for just 33 years, but his impact has shaped nations, cultures, calendars, and eternity. Jesus didn't hold political office, own wealth, or travel extensively, but His love, sacrifice, and servant leadership changed the course of human history.

He healed the broken, fed the hungry, restored dignity to the outcast, and taught radical truths that challenged the religious systems of the day. But most of all, he gave his life. He paid a price none of us could pay so that we could live free. His resurrection wasn't just a moment—it was the ultimate act of Legacy: defeating death and offering life to all.

And today, over 2,000 years later, His name is still being preached, lives are still being transformed, and hope is still being found in his story. That's Legacy. It's not measured by what you gather, but by what you give.

We all have a 'record' to break—not someone else's, but our own. Every year, every season, every assignment is an opportunity to build upon what was. To go further. To reach higher. To dig deeper.

Your life is the most powerful message you will ever preach. Your decisions, your diligence, your disciplines—they all echo beyond you.

Legacy isn't just about creating wealth. It's about creating wisdom. It's about creating systems and structures so those coming after you don't have to start from scratch. It's about mentorship. It's about pouring into people when no one's watching. It's about faithfulness.

When you realise that Legacy is bigger than you, you live differently, give differently, and serve differently. God wants you to expand your vision—not for ego, but for impact. There are generations connected to your obedience. There are movements locked inside your 'yes'.

It's not about how impressive your life looks—it's about how impactful your life is. It's about multiplying your gifts and sharing your platform so others can rise, too.

You may never meet the people your legacy impacts, but that's the beauty of Legacy—it outlives you.

A Final Challenge

As you turn the last pages of this book, I want to challenge you: don't just be inspired. Be ignited.

Don't just read about Legacy—live it.

Ask Yourself and Journal

What mark am I leaving?

Who am I serving?

What seeds am I planting today that will feed someone tomorrow?

Am I living for applause or for impact?

What would my Legacy look like if I wasn't afraid to start?

The greatest record you'll ever break is the limitation you once believed about yourself.

Now go and leave your mark.

Love,

Hayley Mulenda Record

Final Reflection: *The Mic Is Now Yours*

You've read the pages. You've done the reflection. You've stared your fears in the face and still turned the page. That tells me something about you.

You didn't just pick up this book to read—you picked it up to *remember*. To remember the power you carry. To remember the voice you silenced. To remember who you were *before* the fear, the failure, the filters.

Now, it's your turn.

Your turn to speak with boldness.

Your turn to lead with truth.

Your turn to echo what Heaven has whispered.

The mic is no longer in my hands—it's in yours.

Use it to build.

Use it to break chains.

Use it to breathe life into the places that went quiet.

You don't have to be perfect. You just have to be present.

You don't have to be loud. You just have to be *real*.

So go.

Go speak.

Go serve.

Go shift atmospheres.

Because your voice isn't just needed.

It's *anointed*.

See you at the top.

God bless,

Hayley

Resources for the Journey

This journey doesn't end with the last chapter. Here are some tools, platforms, and recommendations to help you continue activating your voice, building your brand, and showing up with purpose:

Speaking Tools and Platforms

- Canva—For creating pitch decks and visual presentations

- Notion/Trello—For organising speaking content, story ideas, and goal tracking

- Calendly/TidyCal—For scheduling meetings and podcast bookings

- Anchor/Spotify for Podcasters—To start your own podcast

Personal Growth Reads

- *Start With Why*—Simon Sinek

- *You Owe You*—Dr Eric Thomas

- *The Purpose Driven Life*—Rick Warren

- *Believe Bigger*—Marshawn Evans Daniels

- *The 21 Irrefutable Laws of Leadership*—John C. Maxwell

- *In Pursuit of Purpose*—Myles Munroe

Free Downloads and Extras

Head to www.hayleymulenda.com/speakupbook for bonus journaling prompts, worksheets, and exclusive resources to help you take this journey further.

References

Chapter 1

Chowdhury, M. E. K., Lim, H.-S., & Bae, H. (2014). Update on the effects of sound wave on plants. Research in Plant Disease, 20(1), 1–7. https://doi.org/10.5423/RPD.2014.20.1.001

Jeong, M.-J., Shim, C.-K., Lee, J.-O., Kwon, H.-B., Kim, Y.-H., Lee, S.-K., Byun, M.-O., & Park, S.-C. (2008). Plant gene responses to frequency-specific sound signals. Molecular Breeding, 21(2), 217–226. https://doi.org/10.1007/s11032-007-9122-x

Benedetti, F., Mayberg, H. S., Wager, T. D., Stohler, C. S., & Zubieta, J.-K. (2005). Neurobiological mechanisms of the placebo effect. The Journal of Neuroscience, 25(45), 10390–10402. https://doi.org/10.1523/JNEUROSCI.3458-05.2005

Kaptchuk, T. J., Kelley, J. M., Conboy, L. A., Davis, R. B., Kerr, C. E., Jacobson, E. E., . . . Lembo, A. J. (2008). Components of placebo effect: Randomised controlled trial in patients with irritable bowel syndrome. *BMJ*, 336(7651), 999-1003. doi:10.1136/bmj.39524.439618.25

Chapter 3

Pauline R. Clance and Suzanne A. Imes, "The Impostor Phenomenon in High Achieving Women: Dynamics and Therapeutic Intervention," Psychotherapy: Theory, Research & Practice 15, no. 3 (1978): 241–247.

Jaruwan Sakulku and James Alexander, "The Impostor Phenomenon," International Journal of Behavioral Science 6, no. 1 (2011): 73–92.

Chapter 5

Christine A. Courtois and Julian D. Ford (eds.), *Treating Complex Traumatic Stress Disorders in Children and Adolescents: Scientific Foundations and Therapeutic Models* (New York: Guilford Press, 2013).

John Briere and Catherine Scott, *Principles of Trauma Therapy: A Guide to Symptoms, Evaluation, and Treatment*, 2nd ed. (Thousand Oaks, CA: SAGE Publications, 2015).

Nathaniel M. Lambert, A. Marlea Gwinn, Roy F. Baumeister, Amy Strachman, Isaac J. Washburn, Shelly L. Gable, and Frank D. Fincham, "A Boost of Positive Affect: The Perks of Sharing Positive Experiences," *Journal of Social and Personal Relationships* 30, no. 1 (2013): 24–43, https: //doi. org/10.1177/0265407512449400

About the Author

Hayley Mulenda Record is an award-winning international keynote speaker, best-selling author, and one of the most sought-after voices of her generation when it comes to leadership, wellness, and communication in high-impact environments.

Hayley has spoken to millions across the globe and delivered powerful sessions for world-class organisations including Google, Microsoft, JP Morgan, Meta, MBC, the University of Cambridge, and the UK Cabinet Office. She is trusted by C-suites, government leaders, HR executives, and DEI champions to deliver transformational messages that bridge personal growth with professional performance.

Known for her unique ability to speak with rawness, relevance, and results, Hayley's keynotes are described as *mind-shifting*, *moving*, and *actionable*. She blends storytelling with strategy, helping audiences not only feel something but *do* something.

Her sessions focus on:

- Purpose-driven leadership

- Mental and emotional wellness in high-performance cultures

- The future of work and intergenerational leadership

- Diversity, equity, and belonging

- Personal branding and visibility in a digital age

In addition to her work on stage, Hayley is the founder of:

- The Overflow Network—supporting upcoming business owners in building sustainable success through biblical principles

- Equipped Movement—equipping purpose-led leaders across business, education, and faith sectors

- Speak Up Events—empowering professionals to leverage their voice as a tool for impact and income

Her voice has been featured in press, panels, and boardrooms, not just for inspiration but for implementation. Whether speaking to executives, graduates, or global audiences, Hayley brings depth, clarity, and practical wisdom.

If you're looking for a dynamic keynote speaker who won'tjustshiftyoureventbutshiftyourteam'sperspective, performance, and purpose connect with Hayley here: www.hayleymulenda.com/bookings

Stay connected:

Instagram / TikTok: @hayleymulenda

LinkedIn: Hayley Mulenda Record

Let's Stay Connected

This book was just the beginning. I'd love to keep walking with you.

Let's Connect

- Instagram: @hayleymulenda

- TikTok: @hayleymulenda

- LinkedIn: Hayley Mulenda Record

One Last Ask

If this book spoke to you, would you take 60 seconds to leave a review?

Your words could be the sign someone else needs to finally *speak up*.

Index

2 04